PLOT

OR

POLITICS

?

D1518386

?

?

?

?

?

?

?

?

Rosemary ? **PLOT OR POLITICS?**
James
and   The Garrison Case
Jack   And Its Cast
Wardlaw

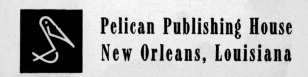

Pelican Publishing House
New Orleans, Louisiana

To our respective spouses, Judson Sterling James, III, and Ruby Wardlaw, who suggested the book and then kept us convinced it was a good idea.

New Orleans Strip Joint

Plot or Politics? is an account of the investigation of the assassination of President John F. Kennedy being conducted by District Attorney Jim Garrison of New Orleans, La. It is not another "assassination book." We have no theories to peddle. We do not sit in judgment of the Warren Commission report or attempt to prove it right or wrong, nor do we set out to establish whether Garrison's investigation is valid. In particular, we do not wish to make any implication whatsover as to the guilt or innocence of Clay L. Shaw, accused by Garrison of having helped to plot the President's death. We are two working journalists, accustomed to dealing in facts, and we have striven to make this book a factual account, and only that.

On the other hand, the authors believe that the issues raised by Garrison are too important to ignore. He has levied serious charges, not only against a leading citizen of New Orleans, but against important agencies of the United States government itself. If he is right, the Warren investigation was a meaningless charade and the public should be justifiably angry at being deceived.

If he is wrong, and is conducting his own charade as some have charged, it may be time to consider curbs on the wide range of powers of the New orleans District Attorney's office.

As writers, we have sought to weave this account around the characters of those said to be involved — Garrison, Shaw, David William Ferrie, Dean Adams Andrews, Perry Raymond Russo, Gordon Novel — a New Orleans gumbo of colorful individuals, some of whom may be villains and some heroes when the final returns are in.

The authors admit to one prejudice — we were admirers of the late President. The truth about his death has a bearing on his place in history — indeed, on the way the history of the mid-twentieth century is finally written. Did a lonely, brooding individual alter the course of history with a rifle shot, or were sinister forces at work to remove this brilliant young leader from the world scene? The question must be answered. Whether Garrison can answer it, we do not know. But whatever doubts the Warren Commission left behind must be resolved.

We hope this book will be a positive contribution to the continuing search for the truth.

— Rosemary James and Jack Wardlaw
New Orleans, 1967

TABLE OF CONTENTS

PAGE

I. ... Of Two Cities 1

II. The Jolly Green Giant 16

III. Through the Looking Glass 31

IV. The Unlikeliest Villain 52

V. "Remember, Perry, the Truth Always Wins Out" 69

VI. "I Can't Say He Is and I Can't Say He Ain't" 83

VII. You Can't Tell the Umpires Without a Scoreboard 96

VIII. I Spy 107

IX. Plot or Politics 121

Appendix: Alphabetical Listing of all persons connected with the probe of the Kennedy assassination by the office of the District Attorney of Orleans Parish.

The authors would like to express their deepest appreciation to:

Their fellow reporters of the *States-Item* for their valuable contributions toward making this book a reality. The editors of the *New Orleans States-Item*, who made it possible for the story of the year to be revealed; particularly in appreciation of their granting us access to the newspaper's files, saving us countless hours in compiling this account, and for permission to use photographs which are the property of The Times-Picayune Publishing Corp. The editors concerned are George W. Healy Jr., Executive Editor; Walter G. Cowan, managing editor; John W. Wilds, City Editor, and William U. Madden, Assistant City Editor; and to WDSU-TV, for permission to use a photograph of Lee Harvey Oswald passing out leaflets in front of the old Trade Mart, and *New Orleans* magazine, for permission to publish the photograph of Mrs. Garrison and her children, and to Herblock for his cartoon in the *Washington Post*.

Chapter One

... Of Two Cities

New Orleans prides itself on being "the city that care forgot."
Dallas, on the other hand, might be termed the city that cares too
much.

Part southern, part southwestern, part midwestern, Dallas
rises out of the rolling Texas plain without really any tangible reason for being there, except that some dedicated Dallasites (as they
are called) decided it would be there, and would grow.

Most cities happen. Dallas was caused. It was caused by men
who went out and got the railroads; it was caused by merchants
such as the Marcus family with the imagination and gall to com-
pete with New York; it was caused by aggressive bankers not a-
fraid to risk funds on a man's reputation; it was caused by newspaper publishers who knew that out-of-town circulation means out-
of-town business.

Because Dallas is prosperous, Texan and deeply conservative, it
has long been one of the most sensitive, self-conscious cities in the
land. Today, in the aftermath of tragedy, the sensitivity is magni-
fied. Dallas has a whopping, massive complex which will alter the
profile of the city for at least a generation.

For this, Dallas can thank one Lee Harvey Oswald of New
Orleans — and others, according to Jim Garrison, also of New Orleans.

"Why Dallas?", Dallasites continue to ask, as well they might.
President Kennedy had visited New Orleans itself in May of 1962.
In spite of intensive planning by the New Orleans Police Department, notably by the late deputy superintendant Alfred A. Theriot
and Intelligence Unit Captain Presley J. Trosclair, security was
lax. In New Orleans, as later in Dallas, the President rode in an

open car, standing, waving, his near — orange tan from Palm Beach accentuating his good looks.

As a target, John F. Kennedy in New Orleans would have been a cinch. If, as District Attorney Jim Garrison maintains, a plot to kill Kennedy came into being in New Orleans, why Dallas?

Bizarre circumstance? Perhaps, even probably, but Dallas has a peculiarly extremist political legacy. Granting, for the sake of speculation, that there was in fact an assassination plot, it is easy to conclude that the intrigue might easily have pointed its way to such a city.

Dallas is the home of Gen. Edwin A. Walker, USA, (ret.), known for his rightist political convictions. Mrs. Oswald has testified that Oswald tried to shoot him.

Dallas is the home of H.L. Hunt, wealthy beyond calculation, an advocate of a republic in which votes are weighted according to one's personal wealth.

It was in Dallas that the far-right National Indignation Meetings were initiated. It was in Dallas that the late Adlai Stevenson was struck by an anti-United Nations demonstrator's sign. It was in Dallas that Lady Bird Johnson was spat upon. There is reason to believe, too, that the preponderance of anti-Catholic literature circulated against the liberal Kennedy during the 1960 presidential campaign originated in Dallas.

In short, Dallas takes its conservatism seriously. It was the quick, almost automatic assumption of millions on Nov. 22 that rightists had perpetrated the crime of killing the President. To these millions, including Jacqueline Kennedy, it came as a shock and perhaps something of a disappointment to learn that the accused assassin was an avowed Marxist. Or was he?

A loner always, Lee Harvey Oswald was very much alone in the political climate of Dallas. Or was he? The Warren Commission which conducted the official investigation of the slaying of President John F. Kennedy says yes. Garrison, among many others around the world, says no. The Warren Commission says Lee Harvey Oswald was a Marxist, probably a Communist.

Now, from New Orleans, the monumental question arises: Was Oswald in fact a double agent? Was he controlled by the CIA or FBI?

With the smouldering cinders of doubt dropping fallout ashes around a skeptical world, the district attorney of Orleans Parish,

Louisiana, rekindled the flame. At the center of the new holocaust stands the towering question: Who was Oswald?

The answer depends upon the respondent. As District Attorney Garrison said at the beginning of his investigation, "Black is white, white is black."

In 1964 the Warren Commission reported that Oswald was the lone assassin of President John F. Kennedy. The blue-ribbon Warren investigators told the world they found no evidence to indicate the existence of a plot. This was supposed to be the last word. But in a world of instantaneous communication–a world which saw the killing of Oswald on live television – the conclusion was too simple for many.

Much of the public's curiosity was unsatisfied. They wanted more. They are getting more. Perhaps more than they wanted. Why do the doubts linger on, and on?

Did the commission conduct itself in such a way as to make America–and the world–think there was something to hide? Have writers such as Mark Lane with books such as his successful *Rush to Judgment* instilled doubts with provocative but unanswered questions?

Are doubts still around because Lee Oswald was gunned down himself by Dallas striptease joint operator Jack Ruby before the accused assassin had a chance to tell his story? Or do the questions persist because there is, in Americans, some deep-seated sympathy for neurotic, congenital losers such as Oswald?

Oswald was a 24-year-old loser with a kaleidescopic background. His life pattern was in bits and pieces, flavored and colored by the national and regional hues of New Orleans, Russia, Texas, Japan, Mexico. He really tried to succeed; he never made it. Most of his life, he inspired sympathy. Perhaps, even at the shocking, tumultuous end, people felt sorry for him – somehow.

Oswald was a product of New Orleans. New Orleans is many things – jazz, pot, pirates, Cajuns, Cubans, voodoo, Bourbon Street, broads, queers. You name it. The birthplace of Lee Harvey Oswald has got it.

Oswald was a brooding contradiction, intelligent but poorly lettered, a self-proclaimed Marxist who found Soviet leadership "sick".

Though the father of small children, Oswald has been linked by Garrison and through a lawyer named Dean Andrews with the "gay crowd" of New Orleans' French Quarter. He was a drifting man of unstable emotions who lingered in the shadows of the cities of the world, dreaming, talking, possibly scheming.

Patrons of a former French Quarter coffee shop visited by Oswald prior to the assassination have been questioned by the district attorney's staff. Garrison has shown an interest in those who frequented the place.

The old Ryder Coffee House was situated in 1963 at 910 Rampart. The building has been torn down and the site used for a motel parking lot.

Investigators questioned the operator of the establishment early in January, 1967.

They sought information on a number of individuals.

A woman who lived above the coffee house but now resides on the Gulf Coast was shown a list of about 20 names by investigators. The Gulf Coast resident questioned said she met Oswald, although not in the coffee house itself.

She said Oswald had come upstairs looking for the manager of the building. Oswald told her that there were a lot of people but "it's really a cold city . . . God, it's cold."

She said Oswald then locked his arms around his knees and shivered.

"I remember thinking at the time that it wasn't really cold," she said.

Oswald is a sharp memory in the minds of many. Memories sharpen as notoriety accellerates. In New Orleans, everybody thinks they remember Lee Oswald. Some remember with pungence.

Kerry Thornley who knew Oswald as a Marine, lived in New Orleans at the time of the assassination. Impressed, he had written the first Oswald novel, *The Idle Warriors*, in 1961. Other novels are sure to follow down through the years. Destiny creates fiction. In this novel, the major character went to Russia. (In October, 1959, only a few months after Thornley's association with him had terminated, Oswald attempted to renounce his American citizenship in Russia.)

Thornley says the main theme of his book is that "you can't train men to be killers, then give them a half-hour lecture, send them to Japan and expect them to be good little boys."

"Stuff like this in the Marines sets up a kind of schizophrenic reaction," he theorizes. "With a person like Oswald, who probably was a little psychotic to begin with, this only makes things worse."

Thornley says he served with Oswald in Marine Air Control Squadron 9 at El Toro Marine Base, Santa Ana, Calif., early in 1959, after Oswald returned from Japan. (Oswald was court-martialed twice in Japan in 1958. Or was he in CIA training? Was he establishing a cover?) Thornley says, at the time he knew him, "He was kind of the outfit janitor, because he had lost his security clearance for being in the brig."

Marine life, Thornley thinks, had a profound effect on Oswald's strange and tormented personality. "I think he became a Communist before he became a Marine, but I believe the Marines only made things worse for him."

Thornley says a mutual interest in books and conversation drew him to Oswald. "He was very well read and I read a lot. We'd get together in the afternoon; he and I and six or seven others discussed politics and religion and such. He said he thought communism was the best religion.

"He had the reputation in the outfit of being a real loser. I thought he was a very intelligent person. This is why I especially remember him. He didn't have any close friends, but he was very witty and satirical in a conversation.

"He was at his best in a crowd.

"But there was always this half-mocking attitude he took. You couldn't tell whether he was really serious or not. He had a wonderful sense of humor. I don't think this was ever brought out in what I've been reading about him," Thornley said.

"He often joked about communism. I remember one time a master sergeant got up on the tailgate of a truck for a lecture of some type. Oswald remarked in a Russian accent: 'Ah, another collectivist farm lecture.'"

At the time of the Kennedy assassination Thornley was working as a waiter in New Orleans.

Thornley says that Oswald's favorite book at the time was George Orwell's 1984, a bitter satire on 20th century trends toward totalitarianism. "I read it at his recommendation. He was always drawing parallels between the Marine Corps and 1984, something I thought funny, seeing as the book is pretty much a slap against communism."

Asked if he thought Oswald a man capable of assassination, a man demented enough to murder a President, Thornley said, thoughtfully, "Well, he was very resentful of the military; he was very much a man who would play the part of an assassin. But I'm not sure he committed the assassination. He never showed any tendency toward violence ... He was more of a talker than an actor. I saw the pictures of his getting shot ... a man I knew, who was sort of a pathetic individual ... seeing him get his ... a slug in the belly ... this got me ... he was sort of a poor soul."

A poor soul? A wretched, distressed, unhappy human being.

Like other, happier people, Lee was born in New Orleans, but his father died shortly before he was born. Memories of the child are dim. Lee Oswald as a youth had few friends. Records reveal he was no great shakes as a student. His mother moved to New York and to Texas, Oswald took his unspectacular tour with the Marines and an enigmatic sojourn in Russia. His original hardship discharge was changed to dishonorable when he applied for Russian citizenship. Then he returned to the States and eventually his native New Orleans. It was April 25, 1963.

A tired, hungry Oswald got off a bus, called his mother's sister Mrs. Lillian Murret, and asked her to put him up for a few days. Mrs. Murret was not told by Oswald that he was returning from the Soviet Union; that he had a Russian wife; that she had borne his child. They had their Russian born child in the United States with them. Oswald arrived in New Orleans alone; he was pretty much alone all of the time. She invited him to her home in a typically southern-urban neighborhood near New Orleans' famed Dueling Oaks where the gentry of another day met at dawn to shoot and stab each other. A pretty and bewildered Russian girl, meanwhile, remained in Texas. Marina Oswald and her daughter June born in the Soviet Union, could only wait for word from the wandering head of the family. Lee Oswald became on the surface a middleclass conformist. He looked for work through the newspapers and at the Louisiana Department of Labor. He filled out forms indicating he was qualified as a commercial photographer, as a shipping clerk and as a photo darkroom man. One personnel man noted on Oswald's card that he was neat, wore a suit and tie and was polite. He was willing to travel on a limited basis and willing to relocate. He seemed, in a word, square.

He even showed interest in his background, in his father's family. He ceremoniously visited the cemetery where his father is buried. He called all the Oswalds in the phone book (there were 21, not all related) and located one widow, Mrs. Hazel Oswald, who had been married to his father's brother. Hazel asked Lee to come by; she gave him a picture of his father. You can't go home again, but you can try. Oswald still had no job. Lillian Murret was patient, even motherly. Lee would spend the day job-hunting (perhaps?) and return to her home. A simple supper. Television. Another day, another nothing. Even Huey Long's state was against a loser. Ineligible for benefits said the employment commission. Lee reapplied. He got one check for $33. On May 9, 1963, less than eight months before John Fitzgerald Kennedy became the most splendid American martyr in a century, Oswald found work. The job wasn't much; he was hired at $1.50 an hour, oiling machinery at the William B. Reily Company, a coffee processing firm near the Mississippi River levee. At least it was work, and the coffee was free. So Lee called his wife in Irving, Texas, a Dallas-Ft. Worth suburb where Marina was living with Mrs. Ruth Paine. He asked her to come to him. She agreed. Old acquaintances, Mr. and Mrs. Julian Evans, had been landlord to Lee and his mother some eight years before. They helped him find an apartment on Magazine St. in New Orleans' well-known, dilapidated Irish Channel. The rent was $65 a month.

Mr. Evans' comments about Oswald are in contrast with those of his wife. Evans says, "His hand was not solid like the average person that you shake hands with; it was soft." Mrs. Evans on the other hand says,"He carried himself so straight."

Mrs. Paine meanwhile drove Marina and June to New Orleans; they arrived May 11. Mrs Paine, her children and the Oswalds toured the French Quarter. After sampling the pungent New Orleans odors and mores, Mrs. Paine left in three days for home.

Oswald clocked in for work at 7:59 on the morning of May 10, 1963. It was the earliest he ever arrived. Later, he became known as a malingerer. A goldbrick, in GI terms. He was to be fired before the summer was out.

A foreman at the coffee plant describes Oswald as "bright, quiet...and often tough to find..." Oswald didn't like his job. He told his wife he was working as a professional photographer. He told Mrs. Paine the same thing. He often spent on-the-job time at a garage next door, thumbing through gun magazines available there.

Says the owner of the garage: "Lee Oswald was not a talker unless he was more or less running the conversation."

But the Oswalds, now reunited, exchanged social visits with the Murrets. Lee's cousin, Marilyn Murret says, "Lee thought he was awfully intelligent but he did seem to love his child very much."

Entering the story at this point is Dean Adams Andrews, Jr.,

Lee Harvey Oswald passing out pro-Castro literature in front of the old International Trade Mart in New Orleans.

Carlos Bringuier, anti-Castro Cuban leader in New Orleans (left) who fought with Oswald over the handbill distribution, and Edward S. Butler, director of the Information Council of the Americas, who debated about communism with Oswald on a New Orleans radio program.

HANDS OFF CUBA!

Join the Fair Play for Cuba Committee

NEW ORLEANS CHARTER MEMBER BRANCH

Free Literature, Lectures

LOCATION:

L. H. OSWALD
4907 MAGAZINE
NEW ORLEANS, LA.

VERYONE WELCOME!

mple of handbill distributed by Oswald in New Orleans in the summer of
33.

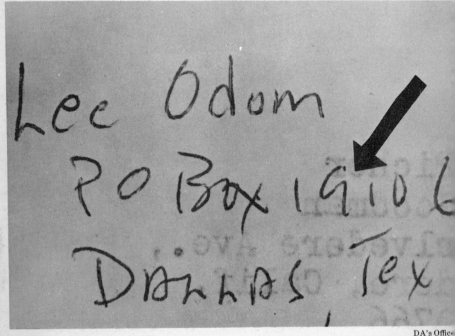

matrie

ark.

W. S. OSWAld
6 ELMEER ST.
MCTRIC

K. Oswald
09 SiERA DR
DENTON, TEXAS

K450267
0-76-1

БА 1206
АА 19106

ОСТАНКИН
ВЛОК '6'

ОВид москва
КОЛ ПАЧН ий пер.

Page from notebook of Oswald, Warren Commission Exhibits page 58, Vol
XVI

Lee Odom
P O Box 19106
DALLAS Tex

Page from an address book of Clay Shaw, taken from the Shaw residence after
his arrest. District Attorney Garrison says these numbers are a coded version
of Jack Ruby's Dallas telephone number.

attorney, bon vivant, persistent wearer of dark glasses and a non-plussed expression. Sometime during May, according to Andrews, Oswald visited his law office seeking advice on his service discharge, his citizenship, and other legal problems. Andrews told the Warren Commission that Oswald came to his office in the company of homosexuals.

Also in May, Oswald wrote the Fair Play for Cuba committee over the name Lee Osborne. He ordered 1,000 copies of a "Hands Off Cuba" leaflet from V.T. Lee, national director.

Oswald passed these leaflets out personally in June on a wharf where the American aircraft carrier *Wasp* was docked.

Meanwhile, at home, Oswald's disposition was not good. In a letter to Ruth Paine, Marina wrote on June 5, "A gloomy spirit rules the house. You know that Lee either yells at me or is silent, but never talks."

Then an economic bomb fell on Oswald. After repeated reprimands, after he showed up late or simply failed to show, the coffee company fired him. It was July 19. Lee applied for jobs; he applied again for unemployment compensation.

Early in August, still unemployed, Oswald visited the clothing store of Carlos Bringuier, an anti-Castro Cuban leader. With a Marine training handbook in hand, he volunteered to help train guerrillas.

A teenager in the store at the time, Phillip Gerci, says that Oswald hinted that he was already involved in some type of guerrilla activity and "he said the thing he liked best of all was learning about how to blow up the Huey P. Long Bridge." (The bridge is named after the Louisiana governor assassinated in 1935, and crosses the Mississippi River majestically near New Orleans.)

During his last summer in New Orleans, Oswald took a book from the New Orleans Public Library. Subject: the assassination of Huey P. Long. Research reveals that he also checked out several James Bond thrillers, *Portrait of a President* by William Manchester, and several works on communism.

Only four days after Oswald's visit to Bringuier, Carlos and two Cuban companions encountered Oswald distributing Fair Play for Cuba literature in the central business district of New Orleans. Heatedly, in English and Spanish, the veracity of Oswald was argued.

Bringuier says Oswald said at the time, "Okay, Carlos, if you want to hit me, hit me." Apparently the suggestion was accepted. The resulting fight, which would not have inspired the Marquis of Queensberry, landed all four men in the tank of the First District Police station.

Oswald languished in the cooler for 24 hours, and kept his cool. In fact, Francis Martell, then a police lieutenant, said he was "a very cool speaker...He displayed little emotion and was completely aloof. He seemed to have them set up to create an incident. When the incident occurred, he remained peaceful and gentle..." Oswald left another impression while jailed, this one with Police Sgt. Horace Austin, who said, "It appeared as though he is being used by these people and is very uninformed."Oswald claimed his FPCC had 25 to 35 members. None have been found. He said the president's name was "A. Hidell."

The weird little accused-assassin-to-be pleaded guilty to a charge of disturbing the peace and paid a $10 fine. He was not content with such sparse notoriety. On Aug. 16, he once again was handing out the literature, this time in front of the old Trade Mart, 124 Camp Street, the seat of many Latin American consulates, including the sealed Cuban consulate. Mart Director Clay L. Shaw, who speaks fluent Spanish, says he did not see Oswald then. He also says he never knew him. Garrison says otherwise.

Another figure in the Garrison probe who contended, until death sealed his lips, he never knew Oswald was David William Ferrie. Garrison contends Ferrie was a key figure in the assassination plot along with Oswald and Shaw, who was indicted for conspiracy in Kennedy's death. Ferrie headed a Civil Air Patrol unit in New Orleans in the mid-fifties. Oswald, then a student, belonged to such a unit for a brief time. Other members of the unit have not confirmed whether or not the two ever met.

Oswald twice visited the city room of the *New Orleans States-Item* in August of 1963 trying to propagandize for Fidel Castro. He was rabid on the subject, strongly protesting the editors' refusals to accept his material.

He also talked to newsman Bill Stuckey who reports:

"On the morning of August 17, 1963, I knocked on the door of the Magazine Street apartment of Lee Harvey Oswald. My reporting specialty then was Latin American political affairs and I conducted a weekly radio program on the subject for WDSU, the NBC-affiliated radio station in New Orleans. A few days before, one of my news sources told me that a man named Oswald was in the city to form a chapter of the pro-Castro Fair Play for Cuba Committee.

"Leftists are as common in New Orleans as panthers are in Lapland. I decided to invite Oswald to appear on my radio program for sheer novelty value.

"Oswald showed me his membership card in the FPFC. He was identified as secretary of the New Orleans chapter. The card was signed by the president of the chapter, A. Hidell. Much later, Warren Commission investigators stated that the rifle that killed President Kennedy was ordered from a Chicago mail order house by one A. Hidell.

"According to the general impression widely held about Oswald — the image of the lonely little nut — I must not have talked to the real Oswald on my radio program that night of Aug. 17, 1963. That Oswald was neatly dressed, of clean-cut appearance, intelligent, an extremely clever debater and relatively well versed in the Marxist view of the world.

"He did tell a few lies, as it turned out, and concealed the fact that he had lived in Russia for several years. Yet it did not matter. On a WDSU radio debate, which followed on Aug. 23, he admitted it, at least superficially."

On August 17, 1963, when Stuckey interviewed Oswald on WDSU radio, New Orleans, Oswald said, "I and the Fair Play for Cuba Committee do think that the United States government, through certain agencies, namely the State Department and the CIA, has made monumental mistakes with Cuba. . . mistakes which are pushing Cuba into the sphere of activity of, let's say, a very dogmatic Communist country as China is." Edward S. Butler, executive director of the strongly anti-Communist Information Council of the Americas (INCA) who was on this radio debate has described Oswald as "a perfect example of a left-wing extremist."

There are other conflicting Oswald reports. The Cuban owner of a Cuban bar on New Orleans' waterfront says Oswald was in his place about 2 a. m. once in September, 1963, drunk, with "Latinos."

Marina Oswald says it just isn't so: she claims the only night her husband stayed out that late, he was in jail. Yet home was not entirely sweetness and light. By this time, she says, marital relations were strained. Once she found Lee crying in the dark, alone. . .

On September 23rd Ruth Paine drove from Texas and picked up Marina and June, the baby, and returned with them to Irving. The next day, Oswald left their Irish Channel apartment, owing rent. No one has determined where he spent the night of September 24. (Marina would pay the back rent after the assassination) On Sep-

tember 25, Oswald boarded a bus for Houston. In his pocket was a
tourist card, good for a 90-day visit to Mexico. He did go to Mexico
City, but he didn't stay that long.

As far as the Warren Commission report shows, that was the
last Oswald saw of New Orleans. But a Garrison witness, Perry
Raymond Russo, testified that he saw a man he knew as *Leon*
Oswald (whom he identified from photos as Lee) in New Orleans in
October, 1963. Lee Harvey Oswald was supposed to be in Mexico at
that time, and his presence there is fairly well documented in Warren Commission testimony.

Oswald then went to Dallas in November 1963. He began working in the book depository from which the Warren Commission
says he fired the shot on Nov. 22 which killed President Kennedy.

After the President was shot, Oswald was arrested and two
days later was shot to death by Ruby. This story is too well known
to bear retelling.

Between the President's death and that of Oswald, New Orleans attorney Andrews was contacted by a mysterious "Clay Bertrand" who asked him to defend Oswald. Oswald's demise made
that question moot, and the Warren Commission said it never was
able to locate Bertrand. Garrison charges that this was an alias for
Clay Shaw, a claim Shaw denies.

But New Orleans district attorney Jim Garrison says, "I have
no reason to believe that Lee Harvey Oswald killed anybody in Dallas on November 22, 1963."

Garrison contends that Oswald was not a pro-Castro agent at
all, but was working within these groups for the CIA. And Garrison
links him with other figures in his case, including Ruby, Ferrie,
and Shaw.

The links to Ferrie and also Shaw are based on the testimony of
a young insurance agent Perry Russo who describes Oswald as
physically dirty and bearded. Nobody else who knew Oswald in
New Orleans describes him that way.

Were there two Oswalds? Was there only one but was he a man
leading a double life? Was the double life connected with Federal
agent activities? Or was he a schizophrenic, indulging his split
personality?

Was Oswald a Communist trying to infiltrate the anti-Red
groups, as Bringuier claims? Was it the other way around, as Garrison claims? Or was he changing faces simply trying to find one
that would find him some friends?

Bill Stuckey, an expert on Latin American affairs, knew Oswald well. He says "he was a nice guy. I liked him. I felt sorry for him, too."

If there was a plot and Oswald was its "patsy", as Garrison claims, there may be reason for even more people to feel sorry for Oswald.

Chapter Two

The Jolly Green Giant

District attorneys are always running for governor. This is one of the hoary, time-tested adages of the newspaper trade, ranking only a little below "If a man bites a dog, it's news" or "don't write on the back of the goddam paper." That DAs are DAs only as a step on the road to the governor's mansion is one of the maxims drilled into the head of a cub from his first tussle with a typewriter.

When a relatively obscure Louisiana DA named Jim Garrison came into national prominence early in 1967 and the world's communications media began flooding New Orleans with their representatives, many of the talented journalists from outside took a quick look at the situation and drew the following, seemingly logical conclusion:

A. Here's an aggressive, handsome, fairly young DA who has somehow stumbled onto a national news story of bombshell proportions.

B. This man operates in a flamboyant, headline-grabbing manner common to politicians on the make.

C. The DA's headlong jump into the publicity mills coincides with a year in which Louisiana elects a governor and other state officials.

Therefore, ipso facto, Q.E.D., here's your candidate for governor, and here's a handy explanation for an otherwise baffling set of circumstances.

There's nothing terribly faulty about this logic. Early in 1967 there was no way of predicting whether the district attorney would seek state office later in the year. It's possible Garrison himself had not decided one way or the other.

The only trouble with the logic is that it is entirely inadequate to explain the motives of this complex, contradictory and often unpredictable individual.

Nobody claims to fully understand Garrison's motives, but most people who have known him throughout his public career would agree that the man wouldn't go to all that trouble just to get to be governor of Louisiana. He might seek the office, but only as a stepping stone to greater things.

How great is greater? Would you believe Vice President of the United States?

If that sounds just a bit far-fetched, you probably are an astute political observer, but are badly in need of a quick cram session in Garrison 301.

The present District Attorney of Orleans Parish (county) was born November 20, 1921, in Denison, Iowa. He was named Earling Carothers Garrison, but as a fighter pilot in World War II and as a student at Tulane University in New Orleans, where he later earned a law degree, he insisted on being called Jim — not James, no middle initial, just Jim Garrison.

He was so insistent that most people forgot he had any other name, a fact that caused headaches for out-of-town newsmen whose copy desks kept insisting on a middle initial.

Nick Lamberto, writing in the *Des Moines Register* of April 9, 1967, said Garrison is still remembered by Denison residents as "Carothers Garrison".

"That's the only name I ever heard him called," an elderly Denison citizen told Lamberto. "I think it was a family name — his grandmother's maiden name. He was only two or three years old at the time and I don't blame him if he changed it to just plain Jim when he grew older."

Garrison's parents were Earling R. and Jane Garrison. His paternal grandfather, T. J. Garrison, was a prominent Denison attorney who owned an elegant 15-room home and about 1,000 acres of farmland.

The home is now an apartment house.

Living next door to the Garrisons in Denison at that time was, ironically, a family named Shaw.

When Garrison was about three years old, his parents were divorced and his mother took him to Chicago, Denison old-timers recall. Prior to that Jane Garrison had been a high school teacher in Denison.

New Orleans District Attorney Jim Garrison in his office in the Criminal District Courts Building.

They also recall an unusual incident in which Garrison's father reportedly "kidnapped" him from Chicago and brought him back to Denison. Mrs. Garrison's attorneys launched a search and found the boy and his father at the Denison Hotel. Young Jim was taken back to Chicago and is not known to have ever returned to Denison.

The father dropped out of sight and was last reported living in Arizona. Mrs. Garrison now lives in Laurel, Miss.

Garrison has since gone through the legal procedure of changing his name to just plain Jim, but as recently as when he sought elective office in 1960 his official announcement identified him as "James C. Garrison". That was the last published reference in the New Orleans press calling him anything but Jim.

Jim was an unknown quantity when, as an assistant city attorney, he jumped into the 1961 campaign for district attorney.

His prospects did not look encouraging.

He quit the city attorney's office with a blast at the administration of Mayor Victor Hugo Schiro, who had taken over from former Mayor de Lesseps Morrison when the latter resigned to become U.S. Ambassador to the Organization of American States. Garrison could look for little support, therefore, from the incumbent mayor, who was seeking a full term of his own in the same election.

Nor could Garrison count on the support of a "good government" coalition of former Morrison backers who were united behind State Sen. Adrian Duplantier in the mayor's race. They had their own candidate for DA, criminal lawyer F. Irvin Dymond, who will figure prominently in a later chapter.

Also in the DA's race was a young attorney named Frank Klein, running on a minor ticket headed by City Councilman Paul Burke.

Garrison's chief competition was the incumbent DA Richard Dowling, an old-line politician in his 70's who had the support of the Regular Democratic Organization, an established, hardnosed political machine.

Lacking any organizational support, Garrison ran as an independent and managed to secure the backing of the New Orleans *States-Item* and *The Times-Picayune,* the city's two daily newspapers.

Garrison wasted no time on his fellow challengers, but directed his fire at Dowling, whom he labeled "the Great Emancipator" for what Garrison termed his penchant for keeping felons out of jail.

Then toward the end of the campaign, came the first of a series of fantastic pieces of luck that put Garrison in the driver's seat.

Garrison and Klein had attacked Dowling for maintaining a private law practice while acting as DA. They pledged that if elected, they would devote full time to the job. (Since his election Garrison has had his name on two law firm doors).

In a much publicized television debate between the candidates, Dymond was asked if he agreed. Dymond, a somewhat haughty patrician type, huffed that after all HE couldn't be expected to live on the $15,000 a year DA's salary and he said if that's what the voters wanted "they'll have to get themselves another boy." The voters, most of whom wouldn't have minded living on 15 grand a year, agreed. They got themselves another boy. Dymond was shot down in the first primary and Klein met the same fate. Garrison squeaked into second place behind Dowling and the ball game was all but over.

Garrison ran in the second primary with the support of a tiny group which described itself as the "Nothing Group". The group consisted of five young lawyers, including Klein and Garrison who chose their name because they had no money, no political backing of any kind and no past victories to lend their campaign prestige.

In the second primary fight, they put on a TV blitz, making the most of Garrison's looks, which remind people of Perry Mason (Raymond Burr), and Garrison's easy way with words.

He picked up the Dymond-Klein support and won with what amounted to only popular support, the kind of support with no strings attached, the kind of support nouveaux politicians dream about.

Old politicos were astonished at his overnight success and were dismayed when he won the Democratic nomination over Dowling by a margin of 7,000 votes. He then went on to beat a Republican opponent by nearly 73,000 votes.

Garrison became Big Jim in truth as he moved his six-foot-six frame into the DA' office.

He began by turning down hints as to who he should select for his staff and appointed as his top assistants his own political buddies, significantly Frank Klein and D'Alton Williams.

Then he named an ex-cop and pal, Pershing Gervais, as his chief investigator, a move which caused bitter antagonism in some quarters immediately and one which was to cause Garrison no end of frustration later.

Gervais had been discharged from the police force some years back and Police Superintendent Joseph I. Giarrusso made it clear that he didn't like the idea of his men working under a man who had been fired from the force.

During a hot investigation in the Fifties, Gervais had testified that bribes were handed out to policemen on a weekly basis in their pay envelopes "like a fringe benefit."

Gervais admitted he had taken his "lousy $21 a week", but swore he had never "hustled" a dime from anyone in his life. Garrison vouched for his friend's integrity and so did others, but there were many people in the city who were not at all happy to see a man with Pershing's knowledge in a position of potential power.

And, throughout Garrison's first term, he was attacked by his enemies through his Achilles Heel — Pershing.

If Klein and Williams were Garrison's top assistants, Gervais was his right hand — and it hurt Garrison when he had to cut it off.

Klein felt Gervais had too much power in the DA's administrative set-up, more power than Klein had. As a result, Klein quit, reportedly because Garrison would neither limit Gervais' duties nor get rid of him. D'Alton left, too, eventually and went into the private practice of law with Klein while holding a job in the City Attorney's office.

Then, in Garrison's 1965 campaign for a second term, Klein and another candidate, Judge Malcolm V. O'Hara, made a target of Pershing and he resigned under fire to keep from becoming a political liability to his friend.

In the early days of office, though, all was apparently harmonious and Garrison, Gervais, Klein and Williams electrified the city with their anti-vice campaigns.

Almost as soon as he took office, Garrison took aim at the city's sin strip — "The Street", Bourbon Street. Former New Orleans newsman Bill Stuckey recalls: "Shortly after he became district attorney in 1962, he launched a crackdown on homosexuals in New Orleans, raiding "gay bars' frequently, arresting "gay kids"on the streets of the French Quarter. After one such arrest, the *New Orleans States-Item* sent me to the police station to see what the formal charges were. There, on paper, probably was one of the strangest charges in U. S. legal history: "Being a homosexual in an establishment with a liquor license." The drive died down after several weeks. One benefit of it may have been the creation of a body of homosexual informants for the district attorney's office—informants possibly involved in his Kennedy plot investigation." In September of 1962, Garrison said:

"I don't think there is going to be a single striptease joint left by early spring."

At the time Bourbon Street was one peel parlor after another with the exotics cozying up to the customers to buy them expensive, watered down drinks and bottles of champagne between the acts.

Prostitution was rampant.

Garrison didn't close all the striptease joints, but he got the B-drinking and prostitution under control. Several places were padlocked, others closed of their own accord and many others raised the tenor of their entertainmnet.

The Bourbon Street caper got the DA into a long dispute with the eight criminal court judges, who tried to block the funds he was using for vice investigations. He struck back, charging the judges' actions "raised interesting questions about racketeer influences."

The judges promptly charged him with criminal libel and he was convicted and fined $1,000. Had he paid the fine, the money would have gone into the fines and fees fund which is used to operate his office. He confided to a friend at the time that if he had to pay he would "immediately commission a $1,000 portrait of myself to hang in my office." Garrison never got his portrait painted, though. The U. S. Supreme Court, in a landmark decision on the right of criticism of public officials, reversed his conviction.

The DA preened and used his new found political leverage to unseat a couple of the judges who had opposed him. His success drove the rest of the bench into line.

After that, Garrison developed a Midas touch in local politics. He was one of a handful of local officials who backed Gov. John J. McKeithen for election in 1964 over Ambassador Morrison.

In the same election, Garrison did, however, make one of his rare political missteps. Before the campaign really got under way, he announced as a candidate for state attorney general against Jack P. F. "Pore Folks" Gremillion, an outspoken racist who had precipitated much of the trouble in the city's 1960 school integration crisis.

Gremillion had incurred Garrison's ire by prosecuting him on the judges' charge of criminal libel.

His temper apparently cooled, because the filing deadline

Mrs. Jim Garrison is shown here with her children. They are Eberhard Darrow, one; Elizabeth Ziegler, two; Lyon Harrison ("Snapper"), three; Virginia, five; and James Robinson ("Jaspar"), seven.

slipped by and Garrison never registered as a candidate. . .And he never offered any public explanation for his change of heart.

Garrison, instead, devoted his energies to helping McKeithen beat Morrison, who had given Garrison his start in politics years earlier. McKeithen's victory made Jim one of the major state political forces.

In 1965, Garrison easily won reelection over one of the judges who had opposed him, O'Hara. O'Hara, like Dymond, will reenter the story in a later chapter.

Before jumping into his campaign for a second term, however, he indicated he might run for mayor, touching off a comedy of political maneuvers typically Louisianian.

Mayor Schiro, planning on a second term himself, met the challenge with a statement to friends that he would "cut Garrison down to size". Publicly, the mayor dropped a few pointed remarks suggesting that the district attorney's staff might be taking payoffs from gamblers, then turned the city police department loose to make an investigation.

Garrison, then a lieutenant colonel in the Louisiana National Guard, immediately flew back to New Orleans from a training camp and issued what he called his "21-point Manifesto." He raised questions about Mayor Schiro, ranging from the mayor's personal behavior through malfeasance in office to city finances.

Garrison: "I will not rest until I get to the bottom of this."

To offset the mayor's investigation, the district attorney flooded City Hall with his own agents to check every record and file. Daily, Garrison said his probe was "continuing", but with each day the number of his investigators diminished. Eventually, the whole affair was dropped by both sides and Garrison later told newsmen, "I was just having some fun with his honor the Mayor."

In another of his many public rows, he took on the State Legislature when it refused to pass his bill restricting the use of bail bonds. He charged that bribery played a part in the bill's defeat. The Legislature voted to censure him, and there was talk of removing him from office. Garrison replied that "it is a great honor to be censured by this Legislature." Earlier, he had said it was a good legislature, one to be proud of.

More recently, one of his old rows came back to haunt him. When he was cleaning up Bourbon Street, he got himself into a feud with the police department. He implied the cops weren't wholeheartedly supporting his anti-vice campaign.

"The police here are like an army that has a mission to capture an enemy hill. Years ago they went out, surrounded it, and then dug in. They've been dug in for so long that they've forgotten what they're supposed to do. They've made friends with the enemy, and even exchanged birthday and Christmas presents. So why capture the hill and end all the fun?"

Stung, the police suddenly remembered what they were supposed to do. They arrested Linda Brigette, queen of the street's strippers, and charged her with doing a lewd dance.

Now Linda's dance--aside from the fact that she actually has some dancing talent--wasn't a whole lot different from those of her sister peelers, who were not arrested. There were some who suggested that the sudden zeal of the cops in Linda's direction had something to do with the fact that her husband, nightclub owner Larry LaMarca, is a friend of Garrison's.

The matter didn't appear to embarass Garrison at the time. His office prosecuted her, and Linda was sentenced to 60 days in jail. Her lawyer appealed, and the case dragged around in court for a few years. Linda remained free on bond, and continued to disrobe on Bourbon Street for the edification of tourists.

In the interim, Garrison patched up his quarrel with the police and the matter was more or less forgotten. But it ticked away in the background and in the fall of 1966 the time bomb went off with a small bang, followed by an explosion.

In November, the *States-Item* revealed that Linda had applied to the State Pardon Board for a full pardon — a curious occurrence, since she hadn't yet served a day in jail.

Garrison, who had approved the pardon application, explained that "new evidence" came to light after the conviction showing that witnesses disagreed as to her guilt. Besides, said the DA, she is the mother of two children and sending her to jail would be an injustice.

Despite unfavorable publicity, Gov. McKeithen, who was then seeking a constitutional amendment that would permit him to succeed himself, laughed at the matter and sided with Garrison. He signed the pardon and Linda never saw the inside of the Parish Prison. "Pardon me" became a phrase to tease the governor and the city had some fun with both Garrison and McKeithen.

The upshot though was a running debate between Garrison and the Metropolitan Crime Commission, which charged that organized crime influences on the DA's office were involved in the case. Garrison emphatically denied that such was the case.

Garrison, also denied the existence of any organized crime in Orleans Parish. After that, Garrison went into an unaccustomed period of silence.

Newsmen used to dealing with the man were curious.

"Garrison sure is quiet". "Wonder what the Jolly Green is up to now?", "Ya talked to Jim lately?" — these were the sort of questions that began to pop up.

The silence startled his friends among the working press and just plain friends.

It lasted until February 17, 1967, when the *States-Item* revealed that Garrison was conducting a "special investigation".

That's a brief history of the "giant". But what kind of man is he? And his political goals? His philosophy of life?

He likes the Brooks Brothers type of clothing, dirty jokes and good Bourbon.

He hates to look fat and will go on a crash diet to get rid of excess weight.

The DA likes to be surrounded by attractive women and one of the legends about his office is that only good-looking girls are hired as secretaries. The legend has some foundation in fact; Garrison's office has more good-looking secretaries, some young, some not so young, than any other office in town.

He likes to socialize, but prefers small get-togethers. He dislikes cocktail parties with a crush of people. The DA likes to stay up late, sometimes carousing, sometimes just talking, but generally he's an early riser.

Sometimes, he makes friends mad by seeming not to see them. He doesn't see them. He's nearsighted and doesn't wear his glasses as much as he should. He's also astigmatic, which makes his eyes look funny sometimes on television.

One colorful description of Garrison was given by a man who has over the years known him well. He says that the public Garrison is like an actor, a method actor as opposed to one who performs by rote. "You can wind Jim up for his entrance and make sure he knows what his cue is, but you never can be sure he will show up for opening night. If he does make the scene, he may then take his cue, but once on stage he'll change the whole direction of the play as intended."

When Garrison took office, one newsman recalls, "He was as real as Thomas E. Dewey and seemed to share a similar racket-busting mentality."

One Garrison expert says:

"He never does anything unpremeditated."

He's described similarly as "calculating."

And, yet, Garrison's public career is replete with seemingly rash statements and actions. His tendency to fly off the handle in print or over the air without giving himself a cooling off period first is a habit he sometimes will admit gives him cause for regret.

Although he is clever with words and extremely well-read, Garrison has not met with much success in his professed desire to become a writer, indicating, perhaps, a trait which some of his detractors — and friends — describe as "a streak of laziness a mile wide."

Garrison does spend a good deal of his time relaxing at the New Orleans Athletic Club and at well-known night spots such as the Playboy Club and he does take every opportunity to travel to such spas as Las Vegas, Palm Springs and Phoenix.

If Garrison is lazy, though, he doesn't work at it. Although he doesn't spend too much time in his office at the 30-year-old Criminal District Courts Building, a fact which gives his enemies fuel for more rumors, he does work at home.

Both of us, as reporters, have first hand knowledge that while Garrison does not maintain regular office hours, he can be found working at home, seemingly undisturbed by the patter of five pairs of little feet.

His periods of relative inactivity when he devotes most of his time to the good life have fallen between periods when he has driven himself to the brink of collapse.

Garrison has a tremendous, dry sense of humor.

Speaking of McKeithen during a period when they were having a spat over political patronage, he said: "You always know John wants something when he invites you up to the mansion to spend the night, then sends you home with a box of peaches."

Once when Mayor Schiro was wavering on a political decision, Garrison issued a statement beginning: "Not since Hamlet tried to decide whether or not to stab the King of Denmark has there been so agonizing a political decision."

His closest friends say, though, that you never know how Garrison himself will take a joke.

A chess player, Garrison seems to be moving words around like pawns when you try to pin him down on his views by checking current statements against past ones.

He keeps bobbing up on the liberal side of some issues, the conservative side of others.

When the vice squad tried to ban James Baldwin's novel, "Another Country" at a local bookstore, Garrison rose up in righteous anger and refused to prosecute, damning censorship.

In the spring of 1965 Garrison said in an article for a law quarterly: "It may well turn out, in the course of time, that our expanding concept of the fair trial, of the rights of the defendent against the state, may come to be seen as the greatest contribution our country has made to this world we live in."

But a year later, Garrison criticized recent Supreme Court ruling which emphasize the rights of the accused, claiming them as a factor behind an increase in violent crimes.

At the 1966 session of the state Legislature, Garrison backed a tough bill providing the death penalty for armed robbery, a bill which was opposed by the American Civil Liberties Union. The bill finally was watered down to provide a 99-year term maximum.

The social ill that seems to bug Garrison, though, might be called man's inhumanity to man. He has expressed his feelings on this subject in a variety of ways, probably best exemplified a foreword he wrote recently for a book entitled, *Crime, Law and Corrections*.

He abhors the public's acceptance by silence of brutal crimes and stated his revulsion this way:

"That spring evening in New York City when Kitty Genovese was so leisurely murdered, 38 witnesses heard her screams and watched the killer toy with her for half an hour. None of the 38 interfered or called the police. A few were afraid. Most did not want to get involved. One was tired and went to bed. The victim died alone, bleeding at the foot of a wooden stairway.

"These 38 grey mice, peeking from the comfort of their holes, may have been watching the destiny of their own race.

"Dachau. . . Auschwitz. . . Mauthausen. . . Sachsenshouse. . . Treblinka. . . New York City. What is your home town?

"The day may come when time seems to hang suspended, when weeds cover our deserted streets and when the only sound is the arrogant squeak of rat swarms, eager now for their turn at evolution. Someone from a distant place, searching through our artifacts may chance upon a human skull. Perhaps he will pick it up, looking through the goggled sockets at the dusty hollow where a handful of gray tissue once took the measure of the universe. 'Alas, poor man,' he might say. 'A fellow of most infinite jest, of most excellent fancy. Where are your gibbets now? Your thumb-screws and your gallows? Your treasured hates and your cruelties?

"What happened to your disinterested millions? Your uncommitted and uninvolved, your preoccupied and bored? Where today are their private horizons and their mirrowed worlds of self?

"Where is their splendid indifference now?"

His checkerboard philosophy is mirrored, too, perhaps, in the wide differences between those who support him. Some have been from right-wing segregationist cliques and others have been moderates of the establishment. On the other hand, Negro leaders say Garrison has been fair and evenhanded as a DA.

And he ran well in predominently Negro precincts in his 1965 race for reelection. He also has appointed Negro assistant district attorneys.

Garrison, when the cameras are not on him, is a family man with a classically attractive blonde wife, Elizabeth Ziegler Garrison, who is younger by 15 years. They met in the law firm of Deutsch, Kerrigan and Stiles where he was an attorney and she a file clerk. They live in a class neighborhood in a class house and all of their children are good-looking and deeply attached to their father.

Before matrimony, the *New Orleans Item* once called him one of the city's most eligible bachelors. At the time (1952) he was deputy commissioner of Public Safety for the City, an appointive job but his first political post. After his World War II service, he was graduated from Tulane Law School, became an FBI agent briefly and then joined the law firm where he met his wife.

He got into politics through the Crescent City Democratic Association, then the political vehicle of Mayor Morrison. He was a colonel on the staff of Gov. Robert F. Kennon. In 1954, he became an assistant DA under Severn T. Darden. Three years later, he sought his first elective office, running for tax assessor on the Morrison ticket against James E. Comiskey, an entrenched ward boss. Garrison was annihilated. He tried again in 1960, seeking a Criminal

District Court judgeship. His opponent was Judge George P. Platt, the senior judge on the court at the time of Garrison's altercation with the judges several years later. Again, he didn't make it.

Garrison actually served as acting district attorney for a brief period in 1958 when he was an assistant under DA Leon Hubert (Hubert later was an attorney for the Warren Commission.)

In this capacity, Garrison had to help conduct an investigation of vote fraud charges in a disputed election for district attorney between, of all people, Richard Dowling, who was to be Garrison's opponent four years later, and Malcolm V. O'Hara, who was to be Garrison's opponent in 1965.

O'Hara had announced that Garrison would be his first assistant if he won this race. O'Hara lost this disputed election in a recount. Garrison then became an assistant city attorney under Morrison.

Since becoming D.A., Garrison has never made any secret of his political ambitions. He has said many times in the past he covets a seat in the U. S. Senate. He passed up a chance to run against U. S. Sen. Allen Ellender in 1966, however, presumably because he wisely concluded that Ellender was not to be beaten. However, Ellender is 76, and should he die or resign in midterm, the governor would appoint his replacement. Gov. McKeithen, Garrison's ally, is up for reelection late in 1967 for a term that will run until 1972. McKeithen is almost certain of reelection — making Garrison a good bet as Ellender's replacement when the time comes, (if his agreement with McKeithen holds).

If rumors mean anything, you might believe that Garrison has upped his timetable and intends to seek a national office of some sort in 1968. He's been quiet on the subject.

One other facet of Garrison's character deserves exploration and that is his enormous flair for publicity, his ability to call attention to himself. He likes to say: "If you want to get a mule's attention, hit him with a piece of stovewood."

What Garrison hasn't said, but should have, is what baseball promoter Bill Veeck said in his book, *The Hustler's Handbook*. Veeck advises that the pitchman keep the whole city in such a state of mind that it's asking:

"What's that screwball going to do next?"

That's more or less what people were asking about Garrison when he lapsed into his strange silence and the Linda Brigette case began to fade off the front pages in November, 1966.

In February, 1967, they found out.

Chapter Three

"Through The Looking Glass"

During the last month of 1966 and the opening weeks of 1967, strange rumors were floating around the corridors of the Orleans Parish Criminal Courts building in New Orleans. Garrison, it was said, was onto something big. The DA's investigators were making mysterious trips out of town. Garrison himself became less and less accessible to the press, and his assistants weren't talking—not for the record, anyway.

But if it was a top-secret investigation, the security measures were not up to James Bond standards. In fact, they leaked like a rotten pirogue. Before the end of January, it was common gossip around the courthouse, at the Press Club bar and elsewhere that the DA was investigating the assassination of President John F. Kennedy. And, rumors said, he had evidence that would blow the dome off the Capitol in Washington.

The *States-Item* reporters began to try to run them down. Direct questions to the DA's office brought a "no comment". To a journalist, "no comment" means "you might be right, but you'll have to get your information somewhere else." Therein hangs the fascinating tale of how Garrison's top secret project, to his professed horror, got into the newspapers.

Garrison himself now puts the beginning of his Kennedy investigation at November, 1966, about the time the Linda Brigette controversy died down and about the time the DA mysteriously dropped out of public view. Newsmen accustomed to dealing with Garrison, including the authors, first noticed that he had changed his unlisted telephone number, in the past available to them and some other reporters in contact with him frequently. These same newsmen found it increasingly difficult to get in touch with Garrison at his office. He was always "in conference" and phone calls were not returned. One of Rosemary James' responsibilities at the *States-Item*, in fact, was to sort of keep tabs on Garrison. She had been friendly with Garrison and members of his staff for a couple of years. Jack Wardlaw, too, had worked closely with Garrison on several stories, and had, during the Bourbon Street crackdown, given the DA his first taste of national publicity with an article in the *National Observer.*

When Garrison suddenly became inaccessible, Wardlaw asked Jesse Core, Garrison's political campaign advisor, if the DA were angry about the Linda Brigette matter. Core replied: "I wish I knew. I haven't heard from Jim in weeks."

New Orleans news media are fairly typical of a large city of the 1960's. There are two daily newspapers, morning and afternoon, with the same ownership (the Samuel I. Newhouse chain); three commercial television stations, with news departments of varying degrees of aggressiveness; two major wire services, the Associated Press with a two-state bureau and United Press International with a smaller bureau; a Catholic weekly, a Negro weekly and a monthly magazine endorsed by the Chamber of Commerce.

Most major news weeklies maintain "stringers"—people who work for the local press but moonlight for the outsiders, while *Life* magazine has a full time correspondent. Other national publications deal with local people on a free-lance basis. People working for many of these media knew about the Garrison investigation, with *Life* knowing more than others about what it entailed, but the medium that decided first the information available was enough to warrant a story was the afternoon paper, the *States-Item.*

The *States-Item* had as a matter of general routine two reporters responsible for covering the DA's office, one a beat man on the scene to handle indictments, trials and the daily flow of information and the other a general assignment reporter with the special duty of keeping an eye on Garrison, an increasing force in state and local politics. The latter is Rosemary James. In following this method of coverage, the newspaper was, probably without thinking about it, using an investigative technique common to police interrogators and news reporters when confronting a prickly source of information. It's called the "high-man, low-man treatment". When detectives used it in the old days—before recent Supreme Court rulings—a tough acting cop used real or implied third degree methods to try to browbeat a confession out of a suspect; then the "low-man" took over, with a sympathetic, "I'm-your-kind-of-guy" attitude, offering the prisoner a cigarette and a shoulder to cry on. One way or another, the recalcitrant suspect usually broke down and started talking.

It works much the same in newspaper practice. In the case of the *States-Item*, the "high-man" was veteran police reporter Jack

Dempsey, a hardbitten Irishman who has spent more than 20 years at the courthouse, which is also police headquarters.

Dempsey does not dig out news stories so much as he blasts them out. His ability to extract news from tough cops and court attaches is matched only by his contempt for Jim Garrison (The feeling is mutual). A personality clash between the urbane Garrison and the hard-headed Dempsey was inevitable from the day Garrison took office. Dempsey's friendships and connections primarily are among the old-line politicians whom Garrison fought, and when in his early days in office Garrison began ridiculing the police department, in which Dempsey takes an almost fatherly interest, war was on. It isn't over yet.

No one in the DA's office, as a result of the clash, was inclined to do Dempsey any favors, but at the same time they knew that given half a chance or reason, Dempsey would clobber them.

The "low-man" operation required only a ready ear and a channel by which more or less favorable news could appear in the paper, bypassing Dempsey.

Garrison is fond of issuing statements on various topics of public interest, particularly on bills he is trying to get through the legislature. Dempsey, unimpressed by Garrison's image as the reformer, was hardly a satisfactory vehicle through which to communicate these gems of wisdom.

The "low-man" was not a man at all, but Rosemary, who was able to extract a good deal of information from the DA's office by winning the confidence of Garrison and his aides.

When the assassination probe rumors began to circulate, Dempsey was the first to hear about it, through his old time courthouse contacts. In fact, he eventually mentioned it, in passing, in his column "On the Police Beat" long before the story was actually broken.

As the rumors persisted, the States-Item city desk, headed by City Editor John Wilds, decided that the matter had to be checked out once and for all. Rosemary was assigned to work with Dempsey and suggested to Wilds that if there was anything to the rumors about the mysterious trips, a check of the expense vouchers for the DA's office, which are public record, should produce something. David Snyder, a talented investigative reporter, poured over the financial records of the DA's office at City Hall, his regular run, while Dempsey and Rosemary worked on other angles.

First, Rosemary called Garrison and asked him for an appointment. He said he was busy, what did she want to talk to him about? She asked him, "Are you conducting an investigation of the Kennedy assassination?" Garrison replied, "I will neither confirm nor deny that."

He said he could not talk about that, but invited Rosemary to come out and chat with him and have a cup of coffee when she felt like it.

By Thursday, Feb. 16, the three put together enough information to break the story, and Rosemary wrote it. It was incomplete, naturally, since the probe itself was still developing, but there were enough hard facts to confirm that Garrison was, indeed, conducting an investigation of the assassination and had spent at least $8,000 on it, mostly on trips to such spots as Dallas and Miami.

That day Rosemary presented herself at Garrison's office at 10 a.m. She handed him her typewritten story. He looked at the first page, saw what it was about and handed the copy back to her. Pressed about the information, Garrison repeated what he had told her on the phone earlier: "I will neither confirm nor deny it," Jim said.

Present in his office were investigators Louis Ivon and Lynn Loisell. Garrison changed the subject to an armed robbery stakeout which had netted an arrest and told her he wanted her to get the facts from the two men. She left with the two investigators, and that was that. Garrison never asked her or anyone else connected with the *States-Item* to withhold the story.

The public shock came on Friday, Feb. 17, when the *States-Item*, in a copyrighted story revealed the probe. The reaction was instantaneous and worldwide.

By late Friday, newsmen from around the world poured into New Orleans to find out what it was all about.

The original article, in brief, revealed the travel expenses, quoted an assistant DA as saying the probe was in fact in progress, and said that several individuals (who weren't named) had been questioned and that another was paid money to assist in the probe. Most important, it pinned down the fact that the investigation concerned a possible New Orleans-based plot to kill Kennedy.

The story was solid enough to smoke out a number of other individuals who had been connected with it in one way or another, including several who turned out to be important figures in the case.

The national press beseiged Garrison, but he did not admit there was a probe until the next day. When he said there would be

Officials of Truth and Consequences, a group of financial backers of District Attorney Jim Garrison (from left, Willard E. Robertson, Cecil Shilstone and Joseph Rault Jr.) The organization changed its name to Truth and Consequences of New Orleans Inc. after Dean Andrews legally reserved the original name.

Two aides to District Attorney Jim Garrison who have played key roles in his investigation are Alvin Oser (left) and James Alcock.

Newsmen and police gather outside his apartment where David William Ferrie was found dead on February 22, 1967. Garrison says Ferrie, Shaw and Oswald plotted to assassinate President Kennedy after a party here.

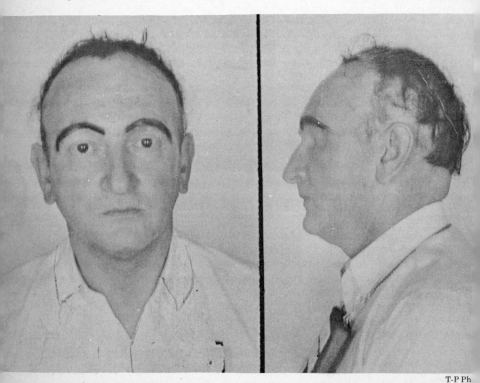

Police mug shots of the late David William Ferrie, when he was arrested on a homosexual charge in 1961.

One of the first persons questioned in District Attorney Jim Garrison's investigation was shipping clerk David F. Lewis, who formerly was an investigator for Guy Bannister.

Layton Martens, who was arrested with David William Ferrie two days after the Kennedy assassination was questioned several times by the DA and later indicted for perjury.

arrests, news media which had ignored the *States-Item* story sent in their representatives.

And, by 10 a.m. Monday, February 20, Garrison's office was jammed with newsmen from everywhere.

Garrison had not been angry about the *States-Item* story on Friday and had told John Wilds as much Friday afternoon. Something happened over the weekend to make him change his attitude to one of fury with the *States-Item* and her sister paper, the *Times Picayune*.

The DA pointedly excluded reporters from the two papers at a Monday afternoon news conference which he conducted in a meeting room of a nearby motel, rather than at his office.

Rosemary was excluded, along with another reporter for the *States-Item*, veteran newsman Bert Hyde, who teased Garrison on the scene trying to make him change his mind with such comments as, "Mr. Garrison, can't I please come in? I represent the *Hammond Vindicator*," but to no avail.

The DA charged that "irresponsible" newspaper publicity had slowed down his investigation and could endanger the lives of some principals. He said arrests in the probe had been only weeks away, but because of the news leak, they were now "months away".

In fact, the first arrest came March 1, less than a month later. Garrison said he would grant no more interviews (but he granted many). He said that the rest of the probe would be conducted in absolute secrecy with borrowed or contributed funds so the newspapers could not continue to track down his spending by inspecting public records. This got some action. A group of some fifty businessmen headed by oilman Joseph M. Rault Jr., president of Rault Petroleum Corp., formed a group known as "Truth and Consequences, Inc," to bankroll the investigation.

Others involved in the group besides Rault, included Volkswagen dealer Willard E. Robertson, testing laboratory head Cecil Shilstone, attorneys Eberhard Deutsch, John Mmahat and Edmond G. "Pudgy" Miranne, real estate executive Harold E. Cook, banker Lawrence Merrigan and many others.

Many of these "businessmen" have political connections of one sort or another. Rault is head of the Rail Terminal Board; Mmahat is a member of the Aviation Board; Robertson is on the Housing Authority, the Mississippi River Bridge authority and the domed stadium commission, and is a close political ally of Garrison and Gov. John McKeithen. Miranne waged an unsuccessful campaign for City Council seat in 1965 with Garrison's support against Garrison foe Councilman Clarence O. Dupuy.

The use of private money to finance a public investigation has raised questions in the minds of many, including one person subpoenaed for questioning who sued members of T & C for interferring with his constitutional rights and privacy, then withdrew the suit. This is a shadowy legal area, but even some of Garrison's most avid supporters expressed the opinion that public acceptance of T & C's activities would be a dangerous precedent.

In the hectic days between Feb. 17 and Feb. 21, Garrison issued a flurry of quotes: "There will be arrests. Charges will be filed and on the basis of these charges, convictions will be obtained."

Garrison made another curious statement, the words of which he had to eat almost immediately. In deprecating the *States-Item's* story, he told an Associated Press newsman: "None of the people mentioned in the press so far are very important in the investigation."

One of the first people to come forward after the story broke was a strange man named David William Ferrie, a self-styled psychologist, private investigator and free-lance pilot.

Ferrie, who contacted David Snyder of his own accord late on the day the first story ran, told Snyder in an interview that night that he thought Garrison would get nowhere with his Kennedy investigation and called it "a big joke". He told Snyder, in joking tones, that he had been tagged as the getaway pilot in a plot to kill the President because of a trip he made to Texas the day of the assassination.

He and two companions, Alvin Beauboeuf and Layton Martens, were arrested in New Orleans by the DA's office 72 hours after the assassination.

It developed that Ferrie had not gone to Dallas at all, but to Houston. Layton Martens says he wasn't on the Texas trip at all, that the second man was named Melvin Coffey. Martens was Ferrie's roommate at the time and was with Beauboeuf at Ferrie's apartment when they were arrested. The arrest got Ferrie's name, obscurely and spelled incorrectly, in the Warren Commission report.

Ferrie told Snyder that he had been harrassed by Garrison's office, but the DA said he wasn't important.

Ferrie, however, had been kept under surveillance by the DA's staff for at least two months before Garrison's investigation was made public. The DA's men established a 24-hour surveillance station in the basement of a house across the street from Ferrie's apartment building, where they set up motion picture cameras to record the movements in and out of Ferrie's building.

By February 22, developments in the probe had come to a standstill. The national and international newsmen, somewhat baffled by Garrison's free-wheeling manner, took him at his word there would be no more interviews and began to drift out of town.

They had to come back in a hurry.

Shortly after noon February 22, news came crackling over the police radio that there was a "homicide" at 3330 Louisiana Avenue Parkway, Ferrie's address.

Ferrie had been found dead in bed, nude, under a sheet and blanket. He was last seen alive at 4 a.m. that day by *Washington Post* reporter George Lardner, who had interviewed him between midnight and four o'clock. The coroner first put the time of death at prior to midnight, but after conferring with Lardner, he said Ferrie must have died shortly after Lardner took his leave.

To Garrison, Ferrie suddenly became "a man who in my judgment was one of history's most important individuals." He said "evidence developed by our office had long since confirmed that he (Ferrie) was involved in events culminating in the assassination of President Kennedy."

The DA said that only that very morning at a staff meeting, he and his aides had decided to arrest Ferrie early the following week and put him in protective custody.

"Apparently we waited too long," said Garrison.

Among the many persons who have followed the Kennedy case with a questioning attitude, there exists a "Kennedy Curse" theory, which, in broad outlines, holds that anyone who gets too close to the situation winds up dying a mysterious death. The chain of the theory begins, of course, with the slaying of Oswald by Jack Ruby before Oswald could tell his own story. (The originator of the theory was Penn Jones, Editor of the *Midlothian Mirror*, a small Texas paper). It has been picked up by others, including *Ramparts* magazine, and the theory extends through the deaths of persons with various connections (some tenuous) with the slaying or its subsequent investigations. All of the people met untimely ends. The list includes, somewhat implausibly, Broadway columnist Dorothy Killgallen, who died of an overdose of drugs shortly after she reportedly vowed to a New York friend: "In five more days I'm going to bust this (Kennedy) case wide open."

The mysterious deaths chain also includes Oswald's murderer, Jack Ruby, who languished and died of cancer in his Dallas jail cell after starting the chain by killing Oswald. To adherents of this theory, the Ferrie death hit like a thunderbolt. Even to those who dislike conspiracy theories, it seemed a weird time for the man to die.

The death of Ferrie and Garrison's investigation caused renewed interest in the death of Henry Killam, who died of a slashed throat in Pensacola March 17, 1964. Killam's brother, Earl, asked Florida authorities to reopen the investigation of the death because of Garrison's probe. He told police his brother had been harassed by "agents" of an unspecified type and had been forced to flee Dallas. The dead man's wife, Wanda Killam, told newsmen that her husband had been questioned several times about the assassination by federal agents. Killam was once employed briefly as a house painter in Dallas by a man named Jack Carter, who once roomed in the same Dallas boarding house with Oswald. Police had ruled his death suicide. He was found by a broken plate glass window. His brother said: "Did you ever hear of a man committing suicide by jumping through a plate glass window?" Mrs. Killam had been employed for several years as a hostess in a Dallas nightclub owned by the late Jack Ruby.

After an autopsy, Orleans Parish Coroner Dr. Nicholas Chetta ruled that Ferrie died of natural causes, naming the cause of death as a berry aneurysm, a weak spot in a blood vessel which "blows out", just like a weak spot in an automobile tire and leads to a cerebral hemorrhage.

Chetta ruled out murder on the grounds that only a hard blow to the neck could have caused the aneurysm to break, and this would have resulted in tissue damage that was not present. He ruled out suicide, too. Aneurysms are seldom discovered by the person who has one until they break and become fatal. The Ferrie autopsy showed that he was one of the rare persons who had suffered a pervious rupture and lived. There was evidence of a previous, but relatively minor break which had healed naturally. If Ferrie knew about his condition, which is unlikely, he could conceivably have done something to raise his blood pressure, which could have caused a blowout.

However, toxicological reports revealed no drugs which might have had that effect and the man who performed the autopsy, Dr. Ronald A. Welsh of Louisiana State University Medical School, said that Ferrie's private physician reported the man had been suffering from high blood pressure. Dr. Welsh concluded from this information and the anatomical findings that Ferrie died a natural death.

Garrison, though, said he believed the death was a suicide, adding fuel to the mysterious deaths, fears and fancies.

Garrison later made it clear what he believed Ferrie's connection with the assassination was. That revelation belongs in a later sequence of events, but Ferrie's background and personality are a story in themselves.

Ferrie, in his last days, was sick, sometimes frightened and bitterly certain that this world held no justice for him.

His strikingly strange appearance and sloppy physical habits prejudiced people against him immediately. This impression was seconded by what was either a vivid imagination or a penchant for avoiding the truth.

Ferrie had no hair on his body. He compensated with a wig made out of what looked like red monkey hair and pasted-on eyebrows. He told one reporter his hair fell out when he contracted a tropical disease in the South Pacific; he told others his hair was burned off in a bad airplane accident. He wore ill-fitting clothes and was described by a reliable private detective as "physically filthy".

He appears despite all this to have been a rather compelling character. He was a man with a fantastic array of talents and experiences, a sort of latter-day soldier of fortune.

Ferrie was a competent pilot. At one time, as he said, he was a respected "man of means", a pilot for Eastern Airlines. Later, he was discharged from Eastern because of publicity surrounding his arrest on a homosexual charge. He never was convicted on this charge. He earned his living as a free-lance pilot and flying instructor and as a private investigator.

Around October of 1966, Ferrie was hired as an instructor at a flight school operated at the New Orleans Lakefront Airport by Al Crouch.

About a month later Crouch severed relations with Ferrie because he said Ferrie was violating their agreement. Ferrie then approached airport officials and requested that he be granted the right to operate a flying school from an office in the administration building. Simultaneously, Buster Abadie, who had an office in the building, loaned it to Ferrie for his personal use while visiting the airport. Abadie later withdrew the privilege when Ferrie abused it and started flying operations from the building. Ferrie requested

FAA approval of that office as a flight school. The FAA was informed by airport officials that Ferrie had no space in the building and airport officials requested that they deny his application.

After that, Ferrie conducted his classes in aircraft in any office he could find and in the airport coffee shop, until airport officials forced him to stop. His inability to continue his classes worried Ferrie a great deal in his last days.

In addition to his flying and investigative work, Ferrie was an accomplished pianist. He had an extraordinary knowledge of chemistry and physics and knew basic medicine and the human body like his own living room.

He was extremely well read. He listed himself in the city directory as a psychologist and he practiced hypnosis. Ferrie once wrote a long thesis, while employed by Eastern, on his theories of a cure for cancer. His ideas sounded plausible and authoritative; whether they were would be for physicians in the field to determine.

Ferrie once studied to be a priest and was a bishop for an offbeat sect later in life. In his apartment after his death were found an altar, robes and other ritualistic paraphernalia.

He was a Civil Air Patrol leader for a number of years and numerous persons have reported that he had the high school boys under his command then and others in a later Ferrie-formed outfit known as the Falcon Squadron "completely mesmerized".

Oswald was a CAP member in New Orleans briefly, but it is not clear whether Oswald was in Ferrie's group. Ferrie told Snyder before he died he never knew Oswald, but there is some doubt on this score.

According to FBI documents, Ferrie originally was linked to the Kennedy probe by Jack S. Martin, a New Orleans private detective.

Immediately after the assassination, Martin got into an altercation with another private detective, one with whom Ferrie had worked, Guy Banister. Martin was pistol-whipped by Banister.

Also immediately after the assassination, Martin told the DA's office that Ferrie and Oswald were in the CAP together, that Ferrie taught Oswald how to shoot with a telescopic sight and that the two had plotted the assassination.

When Ferrie could not be found in New Orleans the night of the assassination, the FBI became interested and the DA's office began combing the area for him. He, Beauboeuf and Martens were arrested by the District Attorney's office after Ferrie and Beauboeuf got back from Houston.

Ferrie told Snyder that while he was in Texas, law officers including Garrison's men, broke into his home and carted off books, photographs and other material. "They took a substantial amount of my property to Tulane and Broad (Garrison's office)", Ferrie said.

Ferrie did not detail just what had been taken from his apartment, but it is known that the items included:

— A library on hypnotism.

— Several 20-page abstracts on post-hypnotic suggestion.

— Three U.S. passports, which were stamped but which had no names, pictures or descriptions.

— A collection of rifles, pistols and other weapons.

Earlier, in 1961, when Ferrie was arrested in neighboring Jefferson Parish on charges of committing a crime against nature with a juvenile, his home was searched. The search netted, among other things, several rifles with ammunition and several maps of Cuba. A news story August 17, 1961 said that Ferrie had been charged with intimidating a juvenile witness in the case by saying that "a Cuban friend would take care of hime if he didn't sign a paper saying he would not prefer charges."

When he got back from Texas, Ferrie said, he gave First Assistant DA Frank Klein a "meticulous" accounting of his trip. It was then, he said, that Klein had him booked as a fugitive from Texas. Ferrie asked his attorney G. Wray Gill to call the FBI and Secret Service. He had an interview with both organizations and Klein then released him.

Ferrie recounted his story to Snyder and said he had been working as a private investigator for Gill, who was at that time defending underworld figure Carlos Marcello in a federal court case. Marcello was acquitted the day of the assassination. Ferrie said he was in court that day.

After his side won, he said, he and two friends decided to celebrate and on the spur of the moment drove to Houston and Galveston in Ferrie's car.

A second organized crime connection in this aspect of the story is that when Beauboeuf and Martens were arrested, they told the DA's men they were not going to talk until they contacted their lawyer.

They gave them the business card of Jack Wasserman, a high-powered attorney who represents Marcello and some of his associates.

Ferrie's story apparently satisfied federal authorities and it was glossed over by the Warren Commission.

The unusual pilot's background also includes a direct connection with men who were training soldiers near New Orleans for the Bay of Pigs invasion. Shortly before he died, Ferrie denied this but apparently he was lying. A man who knew Ferrie well said that Ferrie was closely associated with Sergio Arcacha Smith, one-time leader of the anti-Castro Cuban Democratic Revolutionary Front in New Orleans. Arcacha was actively involved in the training of soldiers for a Cuban invasion. Ferrie denied ever knowing Arcacha, but a number of people, including Arcacha, confirmed this was not the case.

Arcacha left New Orleans late in 1962, he says, and was living in Houston at the time of the assassination. He later moved to Dallas, where he has lived since for about three years. Questioned by a reporter after the probe began, Arcacha first said he did not remember Ferrie and later changed his story.

Ferrie, Arcacha said, often came to his office in New Orleans to offer his help, to offer his plane, to recruit and train men. Ferrie never came through, though, according to Arcacha.

Other reports had Ferrie dropping fire bombs on Cuba, smuggling guns in and people out of Cuba, actually flying as a fighter pilot in the Bay of Pigs invasion, and forming his own training group for invasion purposes. Still another story holds that Ferrie was the pilot who flew Carlos Marcello out of Guatemala back to the United States, after he was deported in 1962.

Capt. Neville Levy, president of an oil rig and shipping sales firm, Equitable Equipment Co., said he had known Ferrie as a pilot in the New Orleans area since World War II. Levy said that once during the mid-50's, Ferrie and two other men visited him to ask for funds to help Fidel Castro's war against the Batista regime.

Ferrie carried a large Army revolver in his hand and placed it on his lap as he spoke.

"Is that thing loaded?" Levy asked. When Ferrie said it was, Levy told him to leave.

In 1961, Ferrie was reported seen frequently in the company of Arcacha, (a fact which made many enemies for Arcacha in the New Orleans Cuban community because, according to one Cuban, of simply being seen with a "man with a face like that.")

Also in 1961, Ferrie was invited to speak on the Bay of Pigs invasion failure before the New Orleans chapter of the Military Order of World Wars. Present was Jack Knight, vice-president of Equitable Equipment, who said Ferrie was introduced as a pilot in the invasion "who couldn't land in Cuba due to heavy ground fire." Ferrie spoke emotionally about Kennedy's "double cross" of the invasion force and his failure to authorize adequate air cover. He got so rabid that several people including Knight walked out and the meeting was adjourned.

Oddly enough, a man who reportedly knew Ferrie and had been questioned by Garrison's staff was murdered in Miami on the same day Ferrie died, February 22.

Diego Gonzales Tendedera, a Cuban exile and the Miami correspondent for *El Tiempo,* a Spanish-language paper in New York, wrote a story after the mutilated body of Eladio del Valle was found in a Miami parking lot.

In his story he said that del Valle, nicknamed "Yito", was a man he knew well and one who was known well in Miami's community of Cuban exiles. He said that before Fidel Castro set up his Communist dictatorship, del Valle had been a Cuban Congressman and a City Councilman in Havana. According to Tendedera, Del Valle fled Cuba with most of his wealth before Castro took over. In Miami, he set up a grocery store as a front for gathering freedom fighters, procuring guns, grenades, bombs and sabotage equipment. Tendedera said that he frequently visited del Valle and that he met Ferrie in the store. During one six-month period, he said, Ferrie and del Valle were together every day. Tendedera said Ferrie and del Valle flew over Cuba two or three times a week in del Valle's twin-engine Apache to drop incendiaries and rescue anti-Communist Cubans who wanted to escape. Tendedera said that federal agents put a stop to the raids in 1961 by confiscating his plane.

Another story reported that the del Valles death publicly had been written off as a gangland slaying, since he was believed by investigators to be linked with a narcotics syndicate, but said that Garrison's men had located del Valle three days before his death and talked to him about helping them.

More fuel for the mysterious deaths theory.

After Ferrie's death, developments in the Garrison story came thick and fast. At an impromptu press conference February 24, Garrison announced he had "positively solved the assassination of President John F. Kennedy" and would arrest every individual involved—"in the course of time."

Garrison: "The only way they (the Kennedy plot suspects) are going to get away from us is to kill themselves."

And then came the real jawbreaker for quizzical newsmen chewing up the DA's every word: "The key to the to the whole case is through the looking glass. Black is white; white is black. I don't want to be cryptic, but that's the way it is".

The DA did not explain his riddle, and he has often publicly quoted Lewis Carroll, but "though the looking glass" is sometimes used among homosexuals to denote "the gay world".

And finally the most sensational Garrison quote up to that point: "I have no reason to believe that Lee Harvey Oswald killed anybody in Dallas on November 22, 1963." This seemed to put Garrison squarely in the camp of those who say more than one assassin (or would-be assassin) was at work on that Dallas parade route. The quote went far beyond the previous assertions of a possible New Orleans-based conspiracy to the President. The DA later expanded on this thesis.

One of the interesting areas is the story of how Garrison got into the case in the first place. That he is in it at all seems at first a bit absurd. It would appear fantastic that one lone DA could do what the Warren Commission, with its immense prestige and resources, did not, according to Garrison, do.

It seems absurd to think that Garrison's small investigative staff could unearth a plot overlooked by the FBI and the Secret Service, with their vast networks of intelligence sources. And yet, this is the first time anyone with any investigative authority has tackled the case since the Warren Commission closed its book.

If one holds the theory that the commission went into its investigation with preconceived notions and time limitations, refusing as some have charged to hear any evidence to the contrary, then the idea of an independent probe— even by some one with the limited facilities available to Garrison—takes on a certain attractiveness.

A copyrighted article in the April, 1967, issue of "New Orleans", a monthly magazine, reports that it was dissatisfaction with the Warren Report that led Garrison to begin his investigation. This article describes a conversation in November, 1966, between Garrison, U.S. Sen. Russell B. Long, D-La., and Joseph Rault (later to head the group financing Garrison) in which Sen. Long took exception to certain aspects of the Warren Report, the shooting itself in particular. Long believed that Oswald was not alone and there was a conspiracy. Rault, too, expressed doubts.

It was this conversation, the article implies, that got Garrison on the track. Perhaps, though, this conversation merely intensified Garrison's interest.

There is the role of Jack Martin, the somewhat shadowy private investigator who brought Ferrie to the attention of officialdom in 1963 after the assassination.

A *States-Item* reporter, who has spent more time than most listening to Jack Martin talk, describes him "as one of the most interesting men I ever have met".

"He is as full of that well known waste material as a yule hen. On the other hand, he is many times a very competent investigator who has the friendship and confidence of reputable, well-placed individuals. He drinks, often to excess, but bears no real evidence of being an alcoholic. He desperately wants to be loved, and this is his downfall. Often, he wants to please everyone, everywhere so damn much that he ends by hurting the people who have befriended him. He must be taken with a grain of salt leavened by a grain of confidence. If you listen to him for two hours, often you will receive two minutes of useful information. I suppose, to sum him up, he is like a muddy river. You have to use a very fine filter." It's more than just possible that Garrison's staff was using that fine filter on Martin, who knew all of the principals who had been mentioned in the case at this writing and names of others who seemed to belong to the same puzzle Garrison was trying to piece together.

Garrison had also questioned Emile Santana, 31-year-old Cuban exile on probation for a suspended larceny sentence, during the week prior to the States-Item publication of the story revealing the investigation.

Santana, who was sentenced in New Orleans, was under the supervision of Miami probation officer Russell W. Buckholt. He was flown to New Orleans February 14 and flew back to Miami February 17. Santana came to this country as a refugee after the Castro takeover. He had been a commercial fisherman, working first for himself in Miami, then in Caddy, Miss., before his arrest for attempted larceny in the summer of 1964 in New Orleans. He was employed by a repair garage in Miami when he was questioned by Garrison. He has a wife and six children.

Another key to the early days of the investigation was Max Gonzales, an old buddy of Garrison's and clerk in Criminal District Judge Frank Shea's court. Gonzales had the job of becoming friendly with Ferrie, but not in the role of investigator. Garrison didn't want Ferrie to know he was being kept under watchful eyes.

Gonzales, who is a pilot himself, made the acquaintance on this basis and made several flights with Ferrie for friendship's sake.

David L. Chandler, former *States-Item* reporter, playwright, and correspondent for *Life* magazine, a once good friend of Garrison and now "outraged by his irresponsible behavior", got interested in what Garrison was after when he found out that Beauboeuf and Martens had named Jack Wasserman as their attorney. Chandler from November 1966 through March 1967 was in close contact with Garrison's office and doing his own snooping on the side. During Janurary, 1967, Chandler says, David L. Lewis was Garrison's chief witness. Lewis, another person who has done private investigation, was at that time a shipping clerk for a bus line.

The Lewis story is that in late 1962, he was drinking coffee with Banister's secretary, Delphine Roberts, in Mancuso's Restaurant, when Carlos Quiroga, a Cuban exile, came in with a fellow he introduced as *Leon* Oswald. They all had coffee together. A few days later, as Lewis was leaving Banister's office, he passed Quiroga, Ferrie and *Leon* Oswald. Lewis was working for Banister at the time. Then, a few days later, Lewis entered Banister's office and there was a meeting in progress of Banister, Quiroga, Ferrie, *Leon* Oswald and another person. Lewis was told to leave. Lewis told Chandler that it wasn't until Garrison's office started talking to him three years after the assassination that he came to the conclusion that Lee Harvey Oswald and *Leon* Oswald might be the same person or recalled any of the above incident.

Meantime, Executive Assistant DA Alvin V. Oser was looking for a target range across and north of Lake Pontchartrain which Oswald might have used for target practice. In the process, he found the locations of two training camps where soldiers were being trained in 1962 for a second Cuban invasion. He also came across a third training camp near Belle Chasse, La., by the Naval Air Station on the other side of the Mississippi River.

Andrew Sciambra, also an assistant DA, was making the rounds of bars and other hangouts trying to pick up information. Sciambra had once worked at the New Orleans lakefront airport and knew Ferrie from those days. However, he was not assigned to get close to Ferrie.

Chandler said that in January Garrison announced privately that he wanted to arrest Ferrie, but it was felt that he did not have enough evidence to make a case. Chandler said he got to thinking about why Ferrie was released so quickly when he was arrested in 1963. Was it possible, Chandler asked himself, that a fix had been on in the DA's office?

He decided that if he asked Max Gonzales, a direct pipeline to Garrison, he might get somewhere. Chandler said he asked "Was $3,000 paid to get Ferrie released?" Gonzales said he didn't know anything. The next day, though, Chandler was subpoenaed by Garrison's office to appear before the Grand Jury.

He showed up and Al Oser came out with a puzzled look on his face and "told me Charlie Ward (First Assistant DA Charles Ray Ward) wanted to talk to me before I went before the Grand Jury."

Chandler said he went to Ward's office and Ward told him that it was the policy of the office to take all bribery accusations before the Grand Jury, "but Ward says to me he will take all of the information from me; he says he has the power, as a notary public, to give me the oath."

Chandler said that, in effect, he took the Fifth Amendment, saying he didn't have a lawyer with him. Ward asked him what proof he had about a bribe. Chandler told him that he didn't make an allegation but asked a question.

He was told by Ward that if, in the future, he asked any questions about bribes, or made any allegations to that effect, he would be brought before the Grand Jury and indicted for perjury if he couldn't back up his questions with answers. "He also told me to get a lawyer," Chandler said.

Chandler showed up for an appointment with Garrison just steps ahead of Rosemary James February 16, 1967. And Garrison told Chandler the paper knew about the story and was going to blow it.

That was the first that Rosemary or Wardlaw knew about Chandler's involvement, although the three of us and our respective spouses had been in close contact socially and were good friends.

Another *Life* magazine team, however, had been spotted on the scene earlier and the prospect of a national magazine beating the *States-Item* on a local story had spurred reporters on in their efforts.

Garrison said later the agreement with *Life* was merely an information exchange. *Life* was conducting its own investigation at the time.

The breaking of the story locally instead of in a national magazine did not, as it turned out, deprive Garrison of a dramatic national sounding board, but it did throw him off balance with the press to such an extent that he never was able to regain the public relations initiative and project the image he might have intended.

If anything, the national press generally has been downright unkind to Garrison. He has fared somewhat better in news columns outside the country, but the foreign press always has had a predeliction for conspiracy theories and thus was quite ready to react favorably to anyone with a new one to offer.

Such influential news media as *Newsweek* magazine, *The Saturday Evening Post*, the *New York Times*, the National Broadcasting Company, and the Columbia Broadcasting Company have rapped Garrison for his handling of the investigation.

The story might have been pretty much ignored for a long time if it had not been for the death of Dave Ferrie.

The timing was so fantastic.

And many newspapers across the country chose to make it a banner story.

On March 1, 1967, funeral services were held for Ferrie. The scene was heartbreaking. No identifiable friends appeared, only a few reporters. His brother, who had claimed the body and made the funeral arrangements, didn't come. The man, who only a few days before had rated big and bold headlines, colorful writing and long stories, was in his funeral notices relegated to a tiny headline and a few undescriptive words.

There was a reason for the inattention of the press. The same day Ferrie was put to rest, Garrison's case moved into an entirely new phase. He made his first arrest.

Typically, it was sensational.

The man arrested has since been described as "the unlikeliest villain since Oscar Wilde."

Chapter Four

The Unlikeliest Villain

New Orleanians by the hundreds were sitting before their TV sets early in the evening of March 1, 1967, sipping martinis or beer and exchanging events of the day when a bulletin was flashed across their screens.

"Clay L. Shaw, retired director of the International Trade Mart, has been arrested by District Attorney Jim Garrison in connection with his probe of the Kennedy assassination."

The reaction?

A kind of numbing disbelief.

"Oh my God. . ."

"He can't be serious. . ."

"Clay Shaw? Incredible. I won't believe it until Clay tells me himself."

"Impossible."

"The most ridiculous thing I've ever heard."

Although the *New Orleans States-Item* had reported earlier in the day that Shaw had been subpoenaed for questioning, most people assumed that the questions would be about the incident during the summer of 1963 when Oswald passed out Fair Play for Cuba pamphlets in front of the Trade Mart. Shaw had been managing director of the Mart then. The announcement of his arrest was shocking to people who knew Shaw and to others who only had read about him and his achievements in the business world and his contributions to the culture of the city.

"Why would Garrison be arresting a man like Clay Shaw?"

The television bulletin warned viewers to stay tuned for details on the late news show. They did.

Garrison's office had filed an affidavit for a warrant to search 1313 Dauphine Street, Clay Shaw's small, beautifully restored French Quarter home. The affidavit charged Shaw, "alias Clay Bertrand", with participating in a conspiracy to murder the President.

In 1963, a Jefferson Parish attorney, Dean Adams Andrews Jr., told the Warren Commission that a man named Clay Bertrand called him after the assassination and asked him to represent Lee Oswald.

Members of Garrison's staff proceeded to Shaw's home and began carting out boxes of his personal possessions...

A ledger sheet from 1963...

One map...

Three pieces of rope...

One chain...

Five whips...

Two pieces of leather...

One Army cartridge belt...

One black hood and cape...

One black gown...

One black net hat...

One shotgun and case...

One black leather book cover with numerous papers...

One book entitled *A Holiday for Murder*...

Seventeen folders containing various papers...

One green leather checkbook with odd papers...

Twenty-six folders containing various papers and documents...

Three manuscripts...

One Underwood typewriter and case...

One white photo album with pictures, two other photo albums..

Five green checkbooks, one black account book and one green leather journal...

Two carbon papers...

Four paperback books and 12 hardcover books . . .

One brown leather folder containing personal documents . . .

One copy of the Wall Street Journal, Monday, Feb. 6, 1961 . . .

One letter holder, red leather, containing various papers . . .

Three pocket calendars for 1954, 1966 and 1967 . . .

And one calorie counter.

Newsmen and photographers recording the search turned that usually quiet section of the Vieux Carre into a spotlighted center of curiosity. A friend of Shaw's, O. M. Wright, offended by what he apparently considered an unfair invasion of privacy, struck out in anger.

He hit television photographer Irby Aucoin. Aucoin pressed assault charges.

When the news shows came on that night, an unruffled Shaw was shown being led from Garrison's office in handcuffs in the company of his attorney and friend of 20 years, Edward F. Wegmann. The handcuffs were out of place; it looked like Garrison was playing it just a bit theatrically.

The handcuffs worried Shaw's friends, who already were concerned for him.

One friend of Shaw's called another and asked, crying, what she could do to help her friend. Equally distraught, the respondent said, "I don't know. I just don't know."

Shaw had been booked under the Criminal Conspiracy statute in the new Louisiana Code of Criminal Procedure, which had gone into effect less than three months earlier. He had posted and been released on $10,000 bond.

The pertinent section of the statute says:

"Criminal conspiracy is the agreement or combination of two or more persons for the specific purpose of committing any crime: provided that an agreement or combination to commit a crime shall not amount to a criminal conspiracy unless, in addition to such agreement or combination, one or more of such parties does an act in furthernace of the object of the agreement or combination.

"Where the intended basic crime has been consummated the conspirators may be tried for either the conspiracy or the completed offense, and a conviction for one shall not bar a prosecution for the other.

"Whoever is a party to a criminal conspiracy to commit a crime punishable by death or life imprisonment shall be imprisoned at hard labor for not less than one nor more than 20 years."

As the evening of the arrest wore on, calls from all over the world began pouring into New Orleans with offers of assistance for Shaw, for Shaw's circle of friends and admirers extended far beyond the boundaries of Orleans Parish or Louisiana. By early morning of March 2, it was obvious that a considerable segment of the local populace was outraged by the arrest of Shaw.

A woman who has known Shaw for many years put it this way: "People who are builders simply are not destroyers."

Generalization often prove fallacious, but could a man who dedicated his adult life to building and improving the economy, culture and face of his city be the same man who whould plot to destroy human life, the life of a man who worked toward similar goals on a national scale?

Clay Shaw, the first man ordered to trial in the assassination of President Kennedy, is to those who know him but casually a man of commanding appearance — six feet, 4 1/4 inches tall, the shoulders of a football player, deep-toned complexion, silver hair, startling blue eyes — a man you could never mistake for anyone else once you've seen him. He fights weight by dieting and weight lifting. He was once a member of the New Orleans Athletic Club (Garrison's favorite haunt).

His manner is cool, detached, but not cold — he is dignity personified.

To the smaller, but still sizeable, number of close friends and associates, Shaw is all this and much more — a man intensely interested in the arts, a world traveler fluent in several languages, a better than average chess player, a man who has the means to live well and does so, a lover of great music, a builder who took immense pride in restoring French Quarter buildings of historic value.

In the business world, Shaw is given most of the credit for making a success of the International Trade Mart and a reality of the new ITM complex at the foot of Canal Street, the main street of New Orleans leading from river across town.

The Trade Mart, organized in 1947, is a non-profit organization designed to promote world trade, particularly with Latin American, and to increase foreign commerce through the Port of New Orleans.

Coast Cuard I

Overlooking the busy Mississippi River port is the new International Trade Mart, the brainchild of Clay L. Shaw. Below is the Mart's old quarters at Camp and Common which it occupied when Shaw was managing director. It was on this corner that Lee Harvey Oswald distributed pro-Castro leaflets in 1963.

T-P Photo

Clay L. Shaw, right, and his chief attorney, F. Irvin Dymond, prepare to
ater the Orleans Parish courthouse.

Assistant District Attorneys John Volz, left, and James Alcock carry
ized articles out of the apartment of Clay L. Shaw on the night of his arrest.

The original building provided office space for foreign consuls, steamship lines and trading firms and exhibit space for the products of many countries, as does the new one.

The old building, located at the corner of Camp and Common Streets, was the place Oswald stood during the summer of 1963 distributing pro-Castro Literature. The building was even then inadequate and scheduled for abandonment by the ITM. In the summer of 1966 old ITM tenants and others began moving into the new ITM tower, a 33-story building of striking design, which dominates the New Orleans skyline from its riverside location — Shaw's brainchild.

Long a prominent figure in the world of international trade, Shaw made significant contributions to improving the flow of commerce through the nation's second most important port.

It is not surprising then that Shaw's friends, both social and business, were astonished at the news that their associate was the first person arrested in Garrison's investigation.

Shaw's own reaction: "I am shocked — and dismayed!"

Garrison charged Shaw, David William Ferrie, Lee Oswald and others met in September 1963, and conspired to kill the President. He said he had a confidential informant who overheard the conspirators plotting. At a news conference the day after his arrest, Shaw protested his innocence and emphatically denied knowing any of these people.

In Washington, the day after the arrest, U.S. Attorney General Ramsey Clark said the FBI had investigated Shaw and cleared him of any connection with the assassination.

President Lyndon B. Johnson said in a news conference that he saw no reason to reopen the Warren Commission investigation on the basis of Garrison's plot probe.

Attorney General Clark said that Shaw was investigated in November and December of 1963 and "we have the evidence and we can assume what their conclusions are," but he said he does not consider Garrison's case valid. "On the evidence that the FBI has, there was no connection found between Shaw and the assassination of the President in Dallas, Nov. 22, 1963," Clark said. Clark did not say why Shaw was investigated in this connection. (At least three other persons occupying office space in the Trade Mart were investigated by the FBI at the same time).

J. Lee Rankin, the Warren Commission's chief counsel, said that as far as he knew the commission never had heard of Shaw.

Shaw said he was glad to hear he had been cleared by the FBI, that he hadn't known he was investigated.

The Attorney General's remark left everyone curious. Why had Shaw been investigated?

Months later, Clark said he had made a mistake. The Justice Department released a statement June 2, 1967, saying that the FBI had not even investigated Shaw. The statement read, "The Attorney General has since determined that this was erroneous. Nothing arose indicating need to investigate Mr. Shaw." The Justice Department said the clarification had been requested by Shaw's attorneys. "Clay Bertrand," the statement said, "was not identified as a real person. No evidence was found that Clay Shaw was ever called Clay Bertrand."

And, locally, people generally were inclined to believe in Shaw.

"Why would a successful man like Shaw have anything to do with an oddball like Ferrie or a loser like Oswald?" the man on the street asked.

New Orleans is a sophisticated city. In many respects its social and civic cliques are uncommonly tolerant of the more exotic habits of some of their own and Shaw had been one of their own for 20 years.

As a result, the cocktail talk, after an initial indignation, was bemused, and centered more on the "humorous" fact that the district attorney "actually" thought a man of Shaw's stature was involved in a plot to assassinate "anyone, let alone a President of the United States," than on the whips, chain and leather straps confiscated from his carriage house. Several people have said that Shaw has used many of these items for Mardi Gras costumes over the years.

If there was a strange side to Shaw's own private life, New Orleans was inclined to ignore it now, as it had for years.

As one of Shaw's friends put it, "Everyone thought they knew about Clay's private life; it didn't matter. It was his personal business."

Even the most blase types, though, couldn't rid themselves of one nagging thought: Why would Garrison go out on a limb and arrest a man as respected as Clay if he didn't have something?

What is "a man like Shaw" like?

Shaw was considered an easy touch. He never refused a beggar and often lent small sums to unfortunate friends. Back in the late thirties, Clay lent a friend and her fiance $250 on which to get married. They went to Paris. The sum, never repaid, depleted Clay's bank account. He said he was glad he did it because they got to meet James Joyce as a result.

That he loves elegance is evident not only from his own carriage house at 1313 Dauphine, but also from the results of many other Vieux Carre restorations he personally supervised and sold.

1313 is a two-story white carriage house, the sides and rear of which are completely blocked from a street view by adjoining buildings which present an unbroken facade along the street. The whiteness of the masonry house is broken only by a red door with a gleaming brass knocker. Shaw had lived in the house for seven years.

Except for a small kitchen, the whole downstairs is a single large room, with French doors opening onto an enclosed patio with a fountain. The living room has a beamed ceiling and a wall of exposed brick, both white.

A large built-in bookcase and bronze grille doors add to the charm of the room, and two walls are covered with pale green silk, the color and fabric of the draperies.

The polished cork floors are scattered with Oriental rugs and the furnishings are French. Several gold leaf mirrors and a painting which formerly was in Clay's ITM office of a flying Icarus complement the other furnishings.

The red door to the house is echoed in red carpeting on an angular stairway leading to the second floor and deep red seat cushions.

Shaw, who has been called a "one-man French Quarter restoration society", has restored 16 houses in the Vieux Carre since 1949, beginning with a six-room house at 537 Barracks Street. He bought this house for $9,500, spent $1,000 fixing it up and then sold it for $15,000.

Enthusiastic about Quarter living, Shaw takes obvious pleasure in showing his guests the furnishings in his home and his taste is much envied. One prominent business associate has been quoted as saying his wife won't buy anything for their house without consulting Shaw.

Among his restorations are the house where the famous naturalist John James Audubon lived in 1821 and the so-called Spanish Stables on Governor Nicholls Street, which were, according to legend, the barracks of the Spanish Calvary when the city was a Spanish colony.

Shaw created a stir when he installed the first swimming pool in the historic section. The Vieux Carre Commission feared there was a lack of historical precedent for swimming pools. Shaw's first swimming pool was architectually classified as a fish pond with a fountain.

Others, however, have followed his lead, much to the pleasure of apartment dwellers in the old city.

Shaw once told a reporter that the irrevocable rule of remodeling is: "Whatever you figure it will cost, it's too little."

Shaw's activities in this area were an inspiration for other investors at a time when the colorful Quarter was literally falling down. Today, although there is much yet to be done, the Quarter has become a high rent district. He has encouraged others to take the plunge on a shoestring, people interested in the architectural value of the Quarter and interested in making it their home.

Local TV personality Terry Flettrich and her husband Leonard live in a house with a colorful story, called the House in the Bend of Bourbon. At the time they began thinking of buying in the Quarter area, Shaw owned the property.

They loved the house and wanted to buy it, but had to sell their own house first. Shaw told them if they wanted the house, he would hold it for them for a few weeks without a deposit. There was no contract signed, just what you would call a gentlemen's agreement fixing a price on the house in event they decided to buy.

During this period, Shaw received several much higher offers for the house than Mr. and Mrs. Flettrich had offered. When they sold their house, they bought the house at their price and Shaw did not even mention the new offers he had received in the meantime. Only later did they find out about it.

Shaw's work in the Quarter has been favorably commented on by national publications including the *Wall Street Journal, House & Garden, House & Home, Town & Country* and *Diplomat.*

Although restoration has been an avocation with Shaw, it has by no means been his sole leisure interest. After his retirement in October of 1965, he turned to the field that had been his first and probably his greatest love — playwriting.

He left for Europe, where he conferred with the widow of the Spanish playwright Alejandro Casona and obtained permission to translate one of the author's plays, *"The Trees Die Standing"*, into English.

When he returned to New York, the translation completed, he told several friends how pleased he was with the results. He is now negotiating for the English rights to the play.

Shaw is the author of several published plays, one of which, the one-act *Submerged*, is still widely played by amateur groups. The play is about men trapped at the bottom of the sea in a submarine. His idea was made into a film called "Men Without Women". The title was taken from a story by Ernest Hemingway, but the story was Shaw's.

In 1948 he produced an original play, *Memorial*, at Le Petit Theatre du Vieux Carre, under the pen-name of Allen White, the surnames of his two grandmothers.

Another of his early plays, also one-act, called *The Idol's Eye,* has been performed in New Orleans several times. Now he is working on an original play concerning the first Spanish Governor of Louisiana, Antonio Ulloa.

It is a rare opening night in New Orleans — whether it be the theatre, symphony, opera — that Shaw is not in evidence, immaculately attired and frequently in the company of a long time friend, Mrs. Muriel Bultman Francis.

He was very active in little theatre work here as a young man and friends recall how very pleased he was recently when he was proposed for membership on the Board of Directors of Repertory Theatre, New Orleans, a new professional troupe which has government backing.

A native of Kentwood, La., a town of less than 4,000 near the Mississippi border, Shaw is the son of the late Glaris L. Shaw, a former U.S. marshall, and of Mrs. Alice Shaw. They are simple, honest, unpretentious, small town people. His grandfather at one time had been sheriff of Tangipahoa Parish, known as "Bloody Tangipahoa" because of old time family vendettas. His name was Clay Shaw and he was widely feared and respected.

Shaw moved to New Orleans with his family at the age of five. He attended Warren Easton High School in New Orleans, then went to work as a local Western Union manager. Sometime later, he moved to New York, where he took courses at Columbia University and then went to work in New York in 1935 as manager of Western Union's mid-city area.

In that position, he was in charge of 40 Western Union branches.

He subsequently went into the public relations and advertising business on a free-lance basis and finally wound up employed by the Lee-Keedick Lecture Bureau, helping to book lecturers. In all, counting his time studying at Columbia, Shaw says he lived in New York City for seven years.

He says he joined the Army in 1942. He was a 29-year-old bachelor at the time. Shaw, recalling his Army experiences, says that he was a victim of typical Army bad classification and that he was "thrown" into the medical corps as a private.

"I didn't even know what a fracture was," he says. However, the bad beginning apparently did not interfere with his rise in the military.

A few months later he was sent to Medical Administration Officers Candidate School in Abilene, Kan., and came out as a second lieutenant. He was sent to England as the administrative officer with the 127th General Hospital Unit. A few months later, he suddenly was transferred to supply, and made aide-de-camp to Gen. Charles Thrasher, commander then of the southern half of England.

Later, he served as Deputy Chief to Gen. Thrasher when he took over the command in northern France. According to Shaw, his unit stockpiled supplies for the Normandy invasion. Shaw rose in rank to major and was decorated for his services – the Bronze Star and the Legion of Merit from the United States and the Croix de Guerre from France.

While he was busy at supply in Oise Bay Section Command at Rheims, France, Shaw worked closely with another New Orleans man, First Lt. J. B. Dauenhauer, III, the scion of a wealthy family, a Loyola University graduate. (Dauenhauer is the grandson of another colorful Louisiana Sheriff, J. B. Dauenhauer of neighboring Jefferson Parish).

Five days after Shaw's arrest, Dauenhauer was subpoenaed for questioning by the district attorney.

Garrison made a point of subpoenaing Shaw's Army records from the Pentagon. A New Orleans court ruled the subpoena defective, but the Veteran's Administration gave the 42-page report to Shaw's attorneys anyhow, and they made it available to the press.

The DA's actions here were peculiar in light of an earlier incident involving Garrison's own Army records.

During his last campaign, the DA got hot under the collar when an opponent quoted from his record and threatened to put the man in jail.

If Garrison was expecting to find something dramatic, though, he must have been disappointed. The records contained nothing more sinister than the fact that Shaw entered the Army in 1942, received a back injury while in training, and was discharged as a major in 1946. The only real oddity revealed was that this successful businessman was a high school drop-out, going only through grade 11. He left school to support his parents.

Defense attorney Irvin Dymond said Shaw "is very proud of his military record."

A month after Shaw was discharged, he was back in New Orleans as managing director and chief salesman for the International Trade Mart, then only in the planning stages, to be built by Rudolph S. Hecht, Theodore Brent and Herbert Schwartz, all influential New Orleans businessmen.

The Trade Mart building was opened and prospered, renting space. During this period of time, Shaw became one of the principal spokesmen for the port and trade industries, appearing as speaker at many functions. Also during this period, Dauenhauer was hired by Shaw and became his chief assistant.

Shaw traveled extensively in Latin America and Europe, his trips including several to Cuba.

In numerous speeches he praised Pan-Americanism, decried tariffs, urged increased trade with Europe and Latin America, asked businessmen to step up trade with Red satellites to encourage their economies and stimulate their independence from Russia.

He praised the Alliance for Progress and said he felt it would prove a boost to the New Orleans economy through increased trade with the countries to the South.

During his career he was given numerous awards, including the Chevalier de L'Ordre du Merite Commercial by the French government and the Chevalier of the Order of the Crown of Belgium.

In September of 1956, Shaw was appointed acting director of International House, a second major organization devoted to the promotion of trade through the Port of New Orleans, while continuing to hold his ITM position.

He was acting director in the absence of his friend Charles Nutter, who temporarily served on the staff of the House Ways and Means Committee in Washington, which was studying foreign trade at the time.

Later that year, Shaw testified before the committee on behalf of the city, the port and the ITM as an expert in foreign trade. He urged a policy which would eliminate tariff barriers.

After Fidel Castro took over Cuba, Shaw told the Propeller Club in New Orleans that the U.S. must increase trade with the new nations "rising from the wreckage of the colonial system."

Meanwhile, according to an influential afternoon newspaper in Rome, Shaw was a member of a group known as the World Trade Center Corporation.

Three days after Shaw's arrest, *Paese Sera,* a leftist newspaper highly respected in Italy for its news coverage, carried a story saying that the corporation operated in Rome between 1958 and 1962, that Shaw was a member of its board of directors and that the organization was a front for the Central Intelligence Agency.

According to the news article, the company ostensibly was for the purpose of promoting trade through exhibitions. The company, said *Paese Sera,* built a rather ostentatious, palace-type exhibition facility but rarely were there any exhibitions.

The corporation moved to Johannesburg, South Africa, in 1962, where it is still in existence under the same name.

Paese Sera went on to say that the other directors of the company at one time included Ferenc Nagy, who was once prominent in Hungarian politics; a former World War II OSS major, L.M. Bloomfield, who is now a banker in Montreal; a man named George Mandel (who goes under the name of Mantello in Italy), said to be mixed up in attempts to purchase national monuments for real estate development in Italy, and Munir Chourbagi, an uncle of King Farouk. Chourbagi was the victim in a fairly recent sensational murder in Italy. Bloomfield apparently was the major stockholder in the corporation.

Paese Sera said that the corporation, although it had moved to Johannesburg, still maintains Rome ties through a firm known as the Italy-America Hotel Company, now constructing a hotel in Rome.

The CIA allegation made by *Paese Sera* was not well documented.

Shaw, when news of the Italian story was released in New Orleans, told the press through Edward Wegmann that he had never been in any way connected or affiliated with the CIA. He said that he had been asked by his own Trade Mart management in 1958 to serve on the board of directors of the Rome corporation, which he said was to have been similar to the ITM in New Orleans.

In September, 1965, after 19 years of contributions to trade, Shaw retired from the Mart. At a luncheon in his honor he was enthusiastically praised for making possible the new Mart.

At the luncheon, the nationally respected architect Edward Durrell Stone, who designed the building, said:"Shaw is one of the greatest, if not the greatest client I ever had." Trade Mart president Lloyd Cobb said: "Shaw's life is a noteworthy contribution to the City of New Orleans."

The City of New Orleans bestowed its highest honor on him, the International Order of Merit medal.

As for Shaw's politics, those closest to him identify him as a liberal and many say he was an ardent admirer of President Kennedy.

Shaw was not a man publicly identified with politics and author Harnett Kane, one of Shaw's high school classmates and a friend in later years, recalls that he "never talked politics".

Shaw describes himself as a liberal of the old-fashioned Wilson-Roosevelt breed.

Convinced that in the increasingly complex urban societies of our times the old doctrine of laissez-faire capitalism is both unworkable and unfair to great segments of the population, and faced at the other extreme with the tyrannies of fascism and communism, with their crushing of individuality, Shaw feels that only through a modification of the capitalist system, as begun by President Wilson and accelerated by Presidents Roosevelt and Kennedy, can the greatest good be brought to the greatest number of people in the world. He is said to have voted for Adlai Stevenson against President Dwight D. Eisenhower, and for JFK against Richard Nixon.

His particular interest in the liberalization of trade between countries made him a staunch supporter of the Trade Expansion Act of 1962 and he was in 1967 devoutly hopeful that the "Kennedy Round" of trade talks taking place in Geneva would bring some reduction in the international tariff barriers.

Because of the success of the ITM in New Orleans, Shaw has advised groups in numerous cities about the feasibility of similar complexes and he once did a complete feasibility study on that type of organization for Puerto Rico.

On the lighter side of civic endeavor, Shaw took a leave of absence from the Trade Mart in 1953 to plan and execute the activities of the Louisiana Purchase Sesquicentennial Commission.

The year-long celebration culminated in the re-signing of the original Louisiana Purchase agreement by President Eisenhower and the French Ambassador at a ceremony in Jackson Square before 50 ambassadors. Clay also coordinated the Jackson Square reception for General De Gaulle.

When Shaw retired in 1965, he said his goals for the Trade Mart had been fulfilled with the realization of the long-dreamed-of ITM tower. Since then, he has occupied himself with his writing, real estate work, some travel and social activities.

Although he did not drop out of sight, being seen frequently around town, for all practical purposes he had dropped out of public life when his arrest abruptly thrust him back into the public view.

He was not what you would call a wealthy man, but he had accumulated enough cash, real estate investments and securities, to allow him to live comfortably and spend the rest of his days writing.

The arrest abruptly changed his financial picture. A good defense costs money.

One of Shaw's friends says that he had to revise all of his ideas about his future, even though he is confident of winning exoneration from any part in the Garrison-alleged plot. The cost of his defense, says the friend, is going to make it necessary for Shaw to look for a means of supporting himself, instead of being able to devote himself to writing.

Once Shaw was free on bond, the brunt of the action fell on his attorneys. In defending Shaw, Edward Wegmann was joined by his brother William and Guy L. Johnson. Johnson later bowed out of the case and F. Irvin Dymond took over as chief defense counsel.

After some preliminary legal skirmishing in which Shaw's attorneys failed to get the charge thrown out, the stage was set for the first step in the legal process for determining Shaw's guilt or innocence — a preliminary hearing.

At this point, Garrison had three legal routes for bringing Shaw to trial:

A bill of information, a grand jury indictment, or a preliminary hearing.

The DA apparently decided against the first method on the grounds that it would give away too much of his case too quickly. He subsequently did get a grand jury indictment against Shaw, so why the preliminary hearing?

Normally, in a criminal case, it is the defense, not the prosecution, which seeks a speedy hearing—almost as a matter of routine.

Garrison never answered the question directly, but the hearing which unfolded could not have given the limelight-loving DA a better opportunity to engage in dramatics.

Chapter Five

"Remember, Perry,
The Truth Always Wins Out"

A preliminary hearing normally is a minor creak as the wheels of justice begin to turn. It's like the batting practice baseball teams take before the action really starts—interesting only to those standing up there getting in their licks.

Jim Garrison's preliminary hearing for Clay L. Shaw, which began March 14, 1967, wasn't for practice. It was for real. It had more drama and excitement than a hundred real trials. And it produced testimony which, unless disproved, will forever cast doubt on the official finding that Lee Harvey Oswald was a lone assassin.

March is a summer month in New Orleans, and the courtroom was hot—but no hotter than the subject matter at hand. For here Garrison had to meet his first big challenge in his effort to prove a New Orleans based conspiracy culminated in the death of President Kennedy. The first details of how he believed this came about had to be revealed, and the world was waiting. It didn't have to wait long.

The purpose of a preliminary hearing is to determine whether the State has enough evidence to bind a defendant over for trial. In this case, the defendant was charged with criminal conspiracy to kill President Kennedy, a felony under Louisiana Law carrying a penalty of one to 20 years in prison.

It was no ordinary court, either. Judge Bernard J. Bagert, presiding judge of Criminal District Court, decided he didn't want the sole responsibility of judging the case and invoked a little-known court rule permitting him to appoint two other judges to sit with him. He picked a neat balance—Judge Matthew S. Braniff, a long-time political ally of Garrison, and Malcolm V. O'Hara, fresh from an unsuccessful bid to unseat Garrison in the latest election for district attorney.

In the defense corner was F. Irvin Dymond, Shaw's attorney, another man who had tasted political defeat at Garrison's hands. The stage was set for fireworks. No one knew just what to expect.

The courtroom itself looked like hundreds of others—the real kind and those you see in films—typically stuffy, somber.

The action, though, was anything but ordinary.

A battery of defense and state attorneys jammed every inch of space in the area reserved for them. Similarly, newsmen crowded every seat allotted to the press after clearing an electronic "frisking" device.

And it was hot.

Even before the hearing got under way, you knew it was going to be hot.

You could conjure up an image of what it was going to be like inside Section H of Criminal District Court before you ever gained entrance ... Like the inside of a sardine can — a tight squeeze and sticky.

It was hot in the halls. It was hot on the steps outside. And it was going to get hotter.

The perspiration dampening brows, shirts and dresses that day was a result of more than just a hot March day and little or no air-conditioning.

The tension that makes you sweat was there; you felt it yourself and saw it at work on others.

Outside on the wide steps leading to the main entrance of the courthouse, a throng of cameramen — banned from inside the building by the presiding judges — waited, their coats already off, and mopped their faces with wilted linen, smoked, cracked jokes and complained about the weather, all the time their eyes en garde searching for a subject to rush with their cameras.

Occasionally, a television interview or a still photograph of a minor figure in the proceedings would be set up against a backdrop of newsmen and the columned entrance.

Dotted among the clusters of the working press were spectators who obviously had no hope of getting inside the court-room...several women in slacks and shorts...a housewife with her hair screwed up tight in curlers...a mother in a house dress carrying a tiny baby...a middle-aged man with a Brownie taking a picture of his wife, who had an airline zipper bag slung over her shoulder...several excited, giggling teenagers...courthouse regulars taking in the spectacle and generally chewing the fat...laborers in work clothes playing hooky.

Later a hawker with multicolored, bunny-shaped balloons showed up, newsmen rested, sprawling on the grass or sitting on the steps, courthouse employes brought out their brown bags for lunch.

The heat, the picnickers, the Duke's mixture of people, the excitement...It could have been the scene of a summer political rally in any Southern town...Except for the waiting, the anticipation, the big question mark hanging there.

Inside, reporters ambled down the marble hall, brushed by the coffee stand, trudged up the stairs and skirted the newly installed telephones, passed Section H and descended the stairs again, stopping here and there to interview another reporter or just to chat.

Spectators with assured passes to the tiny courtroom exuded delight over their fortune, while those with tentative passes just waited and those with no passes at all complained about the size of the courtroom.

The cameramen saw him first. They saw Clay Shaw and his attorneys coming from across the street and they began to move while Shaw was still wading through Tulane Avenue traffic.

By the time Shaw reached the curb, he and his attorneys were at the center of a churning mob of newsmen. Deputies accompanying him had to shout repeatedly, "Move back! Move back!"

Shaw, with not a comment, with not a smile, moved up the stairs, through a human corridor.

At the entrance, cameramen fell back and Shaw and his protective entourage were ushered into an elevator for the short ride to the second floor, while reporters raced up the stairs in time to catch him entering the courtroom.

He carried a large book under his arm and casually puffed on a cigarette.

The cool dignity of this man, whose physical appearance can only be described as startlingly attractive, remained intact. Only his eyes betrayed any sign of emotion. They revealed pain and, perhaps, fear of what awaited him.

The second grand entrance of the day was made but moments later by Garrison, who startled the world when he flatly stated he had solved the Kennedy assassination.

He surprised the crowd of reporters with his deep-red sensitive-looking sunburn and peeling nose. Garrison, in a good mood, said he had been questioning a witness out in the sun and got so interested he forgot about the time.

Actually, he had just returned from Las Vegas. He journeyed there to rest in the company of Jim Phelan, reporter for the *Saturday Evening Post*, and two *Life* magazine staffers.

Garrison appeared confident, if not jolly, and the giant strode through the crowd with his size 14 feet pacing off the steps at an easy gait.

Inside the courtroom, it seemed cool at first. It seemed cool until you sat down and sat there for a while, arm to arm, nine to a very short bench. Then it got stuffy and then it got oppressive.

The question of comfort faded, though, when the moment arrived.

Garrison had teased the world with the idea that he had a confidential informant and, for days, the newsmen involved spent a good part of their time speculating about who the informer was or doing detective work of their own to ferret out the name of the man.

But the name remained a secret until March 14.

The surprise witness turned out to be Perry Raymond Russo, a Republican and sports enthusiast who had lived in New Orleans until 1967, when he became an insurance salesman in Baton Rouge for the Equitable Life Assurance Society.

Russo, 25, attended both Tulane and Loyola Universities in New Orleans, and came forward in the case only after the death of Ferrie.

He told WDSU reporter Jim Kemp and the DA's office he had known Ferrie in New Orleans in the period before Kennedy was assassinated.

Russo, in the Kemp interview, said he met Ferrie through a friend who was a member of the Civil Air Patrol, a friend who told Russo he was training with Ferrie in jungle warfare to "help bring about more democratic government."

The friend's family had contacted Russo in an effort "to break Ferrie's hold on their son."

Russo graduated from a New Orleans high school in 1959 and coached and played baseball in summer leagues while a college student.

T-P Photo

A crowd of spectators jams the front of the Orleans Parish courthouse during the preliminary hearing for Clay L. Shaw in March, 1967.

Perry Raymond Russo, star witness for District Attorney Jim Garrison ir the preliminary hearing for Clay L. Shaw.

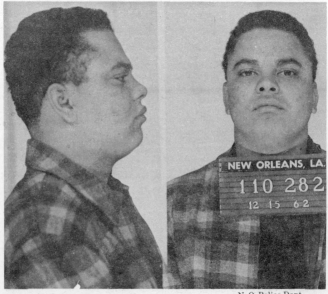

Vernon Bundy testified he saw Clay Shaw and Lee Harvey Oswald together during the summer of 1963. Bundy admits to being a narcotics addict.

This is the touched up drawing of Lee Harvey Oswald which Perry Raymond Russo could not identify as the man he knew as *Leon* Oswald until a beard was drawn on it. Russo said the Oswald he knew was bearded.

James Lewallen (right) and his attorney George Piazza, who was killed in airliner crash at the Hilton Inn.

Besides playing in an all-white league, Russo coached and played outfield for Russo's All-Stars, a white team which competed in (and was champion of) the city's Negro league in 1966.

Russo transferred from Tulane to Loyola and graduated in 1964. That fall, he actively campaigned for Barry Goldwater in the Presidential election.

A Loyola classmate describes him as intelligent but "moody". He said that while Russo campaigned for Goldwater, he was not an "extreme conservative". He would have worked for a more liberal candidate had one been nominated, the classmate speculated.

Russo's name first became part of the investigation when he showed up for questioning March 1, 1967, at Garrison's office, the same day Shaw was arrested.

He was questioned by the DA's office on other occasions, but never was subpoenaed.

As Russo took the stand at the hearing and began his testimony, the pace of pencils and pens picked up, racing for every word.

And quickly, from the lips of the clean-cut, soft-spoken young man, an incredible tale of a plot unfolded.

Under questioning by Garrison himself (it was the DA's third courtroom appearance since his election in 1961), Russo identified a picture of David William Ferrie, and said he met him in 1960 in connection with the Civil Air Patrol. During September of 1963, Russo testified, Ferrie "showed me he was obsessed with Kennedy."

Garrison asked Russo "Do you remember anything unusual happening in the fall of 1963?"

Russo said he remembered that Ferrie carried clippings around with him pertaining to the President and that "there was much talk. . . "

"Around the middle of September, I had occasion to go to his (Ferrie's) house on Louisiana Avenue Parkway. I walked in and there seemed to be some sort of party in progress."

Russo said about ten persons were sitting around drinking.

After awhile, Russo said, there were only four persons left in the apartment. He said he waited around because he did not have a ride home. He identified the other three persons present as Ferrie, *Leon* Oswald (whom he said was a person he had seen several times) and a third person, Clem Bertrand.

This was electrifying. Clem Bertrand was the mystery man

named by the Warren Report as the man who contacted New Orleans attorney Dean Andrews shortly after the assassination and
asked him to defend Oswald. In the search warrant he obtained to
search Shaw's apartment, Garrison had charged that Bertrand
was an alias for Shaw. Now he was backing up that claim.

In the most dramatic moment of the hearing, Garrison asked
Russo: "Do you see the man you knew as Bertrand in the courtroom?"

"Yes, sir." Russo answered.

"Would you point out that man?" said Garrison.

Russo leaned slightly to his left to see around a corner of the
judges' bench, fixed his eyes on Shaw and pointed at the defendant. After a few more questions, Garrison asked Russo to step from
the witness stand and identify the man he knew as Bertrand.

He asked Russo to walk behind the defense table and "put your
hand over his head."

Russo walked without hesitation to stand behind Shaw and
placed his hand, palm outstretched, over Shaw's head. As he did
so, he looked over his right shoulder at Garrison.

A murmur ran through the courtroom, and the court attachés
yelled for order.

Russo was calm; Garrison was calm. Shaw was calm, his eyes
glued on his accuser.

A woman paled, about to faint. She was grabbed by strong arms
and rushed out of the courtroom, where she collapsed, choking.
Coroner Dr. Nicholas P. Chetta administered smelling salts.

Judge Bagert almost immediately recessed the court for lunch.

There was a mad dash for telephones. One reporter, John Lang
of the Associated Press, pulled a muscle streaking down the marble floor. Stories were being phoned and telecast from mobile units
to audiences all over the world.

After the race to get the news out first, reporters and spectators
washed down unappetizing sandwiches with soft drinks or coffee
and jabbered to others. Those who had been inside rehashed a-
mong themselves or related to those left out each detail they had
observed. TV newsmen wiped their faces and combed their hair
and spruced up a bit for their audiences.

For a moment the tension seemed to disappear. Something had
happened after all.

But that moment didn't last long.

Soon, you could hear the questions beginning again.

"Will he stand up as a witness?"

"Can the defense find a flaw?"

"Why did he wait so long to tell his story?"

"Who in the hell is this guy, anyhow, compared to a man like Clay Shaw?"

In explaining his testimony after the hearing resumed, Russo made the following points under further direct and later cross-examination:

—He identified photos of Lee Harvey Oswald as Ferrie's roommate, in September, 1963, Russo said he was then called *Leon* Oswald. However, Russo admitted that *Leon* Oswald wore a beard and he was able to identify the photos only after a beard was drawn on the pictures of the man accused of killing the President.

—He identified Clay Shaw as a man he had seen three times. The first time was during a visit by Kennedy to New Orleans in 1962, when he saw Shaw in the crowd at the Nashville Avenue wharf. The second time was at the party at Ferrie's apartment. The third time was in a car with Ferrie, months after the assassination.

—After Russo, Ferrie, Bertrand and Oswald were left alone in the apartment, the latter three began discussing the assassination of the President, he said.

—Russo said Ferrie took the initiative in the discussion and talked about "diversionary shots." He said there would be two or three people involved and one "would have to be the scapegoat" while others made "the good shot." The three discussed a plan to escape by plane to Latin America, perhaps to Cuba.

—Oswald objected to Russo's presence at the discussion, but Ferrie vouched for him.

—Russo said he saw Ferrie numerous times after the assassination but never asked him about the murder plot discussed at the party.

—He said he did not tell the FBI about the plot because he "was involved with school, which was more pressing to me" and "I never push myself off on anybody."

—Ferrie and Bertrand discussed where they would be on the day of the assassination. Russo claimed Bertrand said he would be on the West Coast and Ferrie said he would be in Hammond, a town about 60 miles north of New Orleans. (Shaw was in San Francisco on Nov. 22, 1963 and Ferrie went to Houston the night of the assassination.)

After Russo left the stand, Coroner Chetta testified that he had administered truth serum (sodium pentothal) to Russo, and Russo was questioned by the DA's office under its influence.

Dr. Esmond Fatter, a New Orleans physician who has experimented with the use of hypnosis in treatment, testified that he interrogated Russo three times under hypnosis. Both Dr. Fatter and Dr. Chetta testified that hypnosis can assist a witness in sharpening his memory and enable him to recall past events.

Dr. Fatter testified that he used the device of having the hypnotized Russo picture a "television screen" and describe what he saw on it. Russo described the party scene at Ferrie's apartment, Dr. Fatter said.

In their final session two days before the hearing, Dr. Fatter gave Russo this post-hypnotic suggestion: "Anytime you want to, you can permit yourself to become calm, cool and collected...You will be amazed at how acute your memory will become in the next few weeks. Things will seem to pop into your mind and it will be only the truth as you saw it....Remember, Perry, the truth always wins out..."

Russo's story was questioned in many quarters, but the first telling blow to its credibility came two months after the hearing in a magazine article.

James Phelan, writing in the *Saturday Evening Post*, reported that he had seen the original report written by Garrison aide Andrew J. Sciambra on the initial interview with Russo Feb. 25, 1967, three days after Ferrie died.

Phelan said the report made no mention of any assassination plot, the party at Ferrie's apartment or any positive identification of either Shaw or Oswald. Yet, in a second memo, two days later, Sciambra said Russo told under sodium pentohal the story he later repeated on the witness stand.

Sciambra, after the article appeared, said Phelan's article was inaccurate and distorted, and that the report Phelan saw was not the complete one.

Whoever is right, Shaw's attorneys were jubilant over the article and immediately asked that Phelan be subpoenaed to tell his story under oath in open court. Phelan stated he would be happy to do so, but the DA's office came back and said that the only way Phelan could tell his story under oath by Louisiana law would be as testimony before the grand jury.

Later, Garrison's case against Shaw was attacked in a one hour special, televised June 19. The National Broadcasting Company claimed that a "Clem Bertrand" does exist in New Orleans and that his true identity was given to the U.S. Department of Justice.

NBC did not reveal the name of the man they claimed was Bertrand, except to say that he is a homosexual and that he is not Clay Shaw.

In summing up the documentary narrator Frank McGee said:

"We cannot say that the murder of John F. Kennedy did not happen the way Jim Garrison says it did. We cannot say that he does not have the evidence to prove it. We can say this: The case he has built against Clay Shaw is based on testimony that did not pass a lie detector test Garrison ordered — and Garrison knew it. One prospective witness admitted he was going to lie.

"Members of Garrison's staff, in trying to strengthen the case against Shaw, have threatened and offered inducements to potential witnesses. The results of his four months of public investigation have been to damage reputations, to spread fear and suspicions, and worst of all, to exploit the nation's sorrow and doubts about President Kennedy's death. Jim Garrison has said 'let justice be done; though the heavens fall, we seek the truth.'

"So do we," concluded McGee.

The NBC show included interviews with Phelan about Russo's testimony and John Cancler, alias "John the Baptist", who told NBC that Vernon Bundy confided to him that he would lie at the Shaw hearing. Cancler who says he is a burgler by profession, also repeated to NBC a story he had earlier given to Gene Roberts of the New York Times. Cancler told Roberts that a representative of Garrison's office had told him the burglary charges against him would be dropped if he would break into Shaw's home and plant something.

Cancler said that he refused and then the DA's staff stepped up its prosecution against him. Cancler's story was carried in the same article with a story told by Parish Prison inmate Miguel Torres, a one-time heroin addict, who said he was offered his freedom, an ounce of heroin and three months' vacation in Florida if he would be "cooperative" in the DA's investigation.

Lefty Peterson, whom Russo named as having accompanied

him to the party at Ferrie's house, said during the show that no one fitting Shaw's description or Lee Harvey Oswald's description was present at the party. Layton Martens said on the air that he knew of no Ferrie roommate named Oswald. He said that James Lewallen, who has been questioned by Garrison, had roomed with Ferrie and was on occasion called "Lew" or "Lee".

Interspersed through Russo's testimony were the names of other people who had attended the fateful party at Ferrie's apartment.

One of these was Sandra Moffet, whom Russo claimed accompanied him to the gathering. After the hearing, she turned up in Omaha as Sandra Moffet McMaines, the wife of a minister. She told newsmen she was something of a "party girl" while in New Orleans and was in love with Russo at one time.

However, she denied attending the party in question and she said that while she knew Dave Ferrie she didn't meet him until 1965. She refused, though, to come back to New Orleans and testify, and Garrison's efforts to extradite her met with solid resistence. She moved from Nebraska to Iowa, which has no extradition agreement with Louisiana.

She said during the NBC show that she was offered clothes and the best of accommodations if she would return to New Orleans to testify for the state.

Russo's sensational testimony left participants in the preliminary hearing so limp that neither judges nor spectators could get their vital juices flowing over Bundy, a Negro parish prison inmate, who testified that he saw Oswald and Shaw talking together on the New Orleans lakefront during the Summer of 1963.

After a hectic four days of testimony, the panel ruled that sufficient evidence had been presented to sustain the charge against Shaw, thus setting the stage for an historic trial.

Shaw observed his 54th birthday on the final day of the hearing, March 14. His present? Being allowed to remain free on $10,000 bond.

One of the most curious aspects of the hearing was the refusal of the three-judge panel to permit the report of the Warren Commission to be introduced in evidence.

Dymond had asked Russo a question that clearly referred to the report. Russo said he had seen the man he knew as Leon Oswald in New Orleans at a time when the Warren Commission investigators claimed he was in Mexico.

When Dymond questioned Russo on this point, first assistant DA Charles Ray Ward objected. He contended that the Warren Report had "never been proven in court."

Meanwhile, at a signal from Dymond, aides had begun toting into court the entire 26 volumes of the report.

Judge Bagert leaned forward to Dymond and said:

"You are going to introduce the Warren Report? You are not serious, are you?"

Dymond insisted that he was, indeed, serious.

"You mean it is your interpretation that you can put the whole Warren Report in evidence?" asked Bagert.

Without waiting for a reply, Judge Bagert turned to his fellow judges and Ward's objection was sustained.

On what grounds?

That the Warren Report is hearsay.

Chapter Six

"I Can't Say He Is
And I Can't Say He Ain't"

A roly-poly cat from New Orleans might have made the big time as a mouthpiece but he was too "squirrelly" to go to Dallas in November of 1963.

As it turned out, it didn't really matter that he couldn't make the scene. His potential client got knocked off.

Dean Adams Andrews Jr., a rotund lawyer who wears dark glasses at all times and talks like an updated Damon Runyon character, has played a major role in Jim Garrison's assassination investigation. In fact Garrison might not have had any investigation or any thought of arresting Clay L. Shaw—had it not been for Andrews.

This man, who until recently was an assistant prosecutor himself, was the first man to mention the name "Clay Bertrand" in connection with the Kennedy investigation. He told the Warren Commission that a man by that name called him after the assassination and asked him to defend Oswald.

The FBI never could come up with a man fitting Bertrand's description, perhaps because Andrews gave conflicting descriptions of the man he knew "mostly as a voice on the phone."

But Garrison since he began his assassination probe deduced that Clay Shaw was Clay Bertrand and then came up with a witness to testify to it. Not Andrews, though. Andrews until recently stoutly maintained: "I can't say he is and I can't say he ain't."

Andrews has been questioned by Garrison and by the Orleans Parish Grand Jury and has twice been indicted for perjury. He was convicted on three counts August 14.

The legal battle over whether the perjury charge against Andrews would ever get to court became confused over the question of just exactly where in his testimony before the grand jury Andrews was supposed to have made false statements.

After the grand jury revised its first indictment document and included a lengthy portion of his testimony and said this was the suspect portion, Andrews and Zelden said that it still had not been spelled out specifically where he was accused of making a false statement or statements.

In the meantime, Andrews has provided humorous relief in an otherwide dead-serious situation. The Warren Report's 26 volumes contain 14 1/2 pages of testimony shot through with colorful Andrewisms.

He relates that Oswald came to him for legal advice about a "discharge, a yellow paper discharge" sometime during early summer of 1963, probably in May.

Oswald, he said, was accompanied by some "gay kids" and what he assumed to be a Mexican man. "We saw him three or four times subsequent to that, not in the company of the gay kids. He had this Mexicano with him. I assume he is a Mex because the Latins do not wear a butch hair cut."

He told commission attorney Wesley J. Liebler that he had received a phone call asking him to go to Dallas. "I was in Hotel Dieu (a Catholic hospital in New Orleans) and the phone rang and a voice I recognized as Clay Bertrand asked me if I would go to Dallas and Houston — I think Dallas, I guess — wherever it was this boy was being held — and defend him. I told him I was sick in the hospital. If I couldn't go I would find someone who could go."

Andrews told Liebler: "I had seen Clay Bertrand once some time ago, probably a couple of years. He's the one who calls in behalf of gay kids normally, either to obtain bond or parole for them. I would assume that he was the one that originally sent Oswald and the gay kids, these Mexicanos, to the office because I had never seen those people before at all. They were just walk-ins."

Andrews, under questioning, said that Bertrand was "mostly a voice on the phone." He gave a statement to the FBI which described Bertrand as about six feet, one to two inches tall, with brown hair, well dressed. When giving testimony to Liebler, he described Bertrand as follows: "He is about 5 feet, eight inches. Got sandy hair, blue eyes, ruddy complexion. Must weigh about 165, 170, 175."

(Neither of these descriptions strongly suggests the very tall, silver-haired Shaw.)

Asked about the discrepancy in the two descriptions he gave, Andrews said: "But, you know, I don't play Boy Scouts and measure them. I have only seen this fellow twice in my life. I don't think there is that much difference in the description. There may be some to some artist, but to me, there isn't that much difference. Might be for you all."

He described Bertrand as "bisexual. What they call a swinging cat."

Andrews also was not too specific about the time of day he got the phone call to represent Oswald. He explained to Liebler that he was in the hospital and was "squirrelly." He had pneumonia and was under heavy sedation at the time.

Asked by Liebler, "Did Oswald appear to be gay?" Andrews replies: "You can't tell. I couldn't say. He swang with the kids. He didn't swish, but birds of a feather flock together. I don't know any squares that run with them. They may go down to look."

Andrews said: "He (Oswald) is not effeminate; his voice isn't squeaky; he didn't walk like or talk like a girl; he walks and talks like a man." Asked if he noticed anything about the way Oswald walked, Andrews replied:

"I never paid attention. I never watched him walk other than into and out of the office. There's nothing that would draw attention to anything out of the ordinary, but I just assumed that he knew these people and was running with them. They had no reason to come. The three gay kids he was with, they were ostentatious. They were what we call swishers. You can just look at them. All they had to do was open their mouth. That was it. Walk, they can swing better than Sammy Kaye. They do real good. With those pronounced ones, you never know what the relationship is with anyone else with them, but I have no way of telling whether he is gay or not, other than he came in with what they call here queens. That's about it."

Andrews' testimony was taken July 21, 1964, at the old Civil Courts Building, Royal and Conti in the French Quarter. He had been questioned by the FBI in December, 1963. Leibler questioned Andrews about his discussions with the FBI. He asked Andrews if "in your continuing discussions with the FBI, you finally came to the conclusion that Clay Bertrand was a figment of your imagination?"

Andrews replied: "That's what the Feebees (his name for FBI agents) put on. I know that the two Feebees are going to put these people on the street looking, and I can't find the guy and I am not going to tie up all the agents on something that isn't that solid. I told them, 'Write what you want, that I am nuts. I don't care.' They were running on the time factor, and the hills were shook up plenty to get it, get it, get it. I couldn't give it to them. I have been playing cops and robbers with them. You can tell when the steam is on. They are on you like the plague. They never leave. They are like cancer. Eternal."

Andrews was called in for questioning by Garrison the same day Clay Shaw was arrested. He was accompanied to the DA's office by his attorney Sam Monk Zelden, a colorful figure in his own right.

Zelden and Andrews are cut from the same cloth—hip, breezy talk, good-humored in adverse circumstances, friendly, funny.

When Andrews wants to make an objection in court, he yells "foul!". Zelden, who looks more like a football coach than a lawyer, talks in frog-like tones and has button-black eyes that go wide with mock astonishment at the slightest provocation.

When Zelden tells you something he shouldn't be telling you, he has a habit of repeating, "I didn't hear that, I didn't hear that."

Zelden almost got into the case on his own. Andrews called him from the hospital back in 1963 and asked him to go to Dallas on the Oswald case.

It was the Sunday after Kennedy died and Zelden and his son were at the New Orleans Athletic Club. They had just finished a dip in the pool when the elder Zelden was paged for a phone call. He answered and was shocked to hear the proposition made by the party on the other end of the line. Andrews was calling from the hospital and asking him to go to Dallas and consult with Oswald. Zelden said: "I was flabbergasted. The lawyer who called me told me he was in a hospital with 106 degrees of fever and couldn't leave for Dallas. He asked me to take his place and to assist him in the trial of the case whenever it came to trial."

Zelden said the proposal almost floored him. "I told the lawyer I would need time to think it over. He told me to call him back quickly as time was of the utmost importance.

"I hung up the phone and shook my head in disbelief. What a decision to make! My thoughts to this time after watching the e-vents on TV and reading the accounts in the press were centered on the tragic event in Dallas, with deep sympathy for the President and his family and revulsion and contempt for his assassin, whoever he might be. Now I was being requested to advise the man who was charged with murdering the President and the Dallas po-

lice officer. My immediate reaction to the proposal was a flat refusal, but I felt I owed it to my friend to consider all the aspects. Suddenly I heard a noise from the bar and when I went to see what had
happened, I learned that it had been reported on TV that Oswald
had been shot. About a half-hour later, I learned he died of his
wounds. The action in Dallas had relieved me of making a decision
in the matter. I'll always wonder, however, what I would have done
had he lived. I'm sure I would have turned down the request...but
it was quite a challenging offer."

Zelden, who was a slashing power runner for the Loyola University football teams of the early 1930's, is a longtime local political
figure and a bitter opponent of Garrison. He sought the DA's office
once himself, but lost.

After being interviewed on television in connection with the
Garrison probe, Monk made a typical Zelden comment. "This is my
last day as a lawyer. I've just signed a TV contract...Now, you
want to hear the real story? Twelve mothers called me up to say
stay off TV...I scare their kids, they tell me."

After Andrews was questioned by Garrison, he was brought
before the grand jury and, with some additions, recalled his testimony to the Warren Commission. Out of his grand jury appearance
grew the perjury indictments.

Zelden contended the original indictment of Andrews was defective because it did not spell out what testimony before the
grand jury was perjurous. Subsequently, Andrews was reindicted
and the suspect portion of his testimony revealed, and it includes
some of the oddest exchanges in American jurisprudence.

Here are some excerpts:

"Question by grand juror:

"Q. Would you state positively that Clay Shaw and Clay Bertrand were not the same people?

"A. I could not do it...I can't connect the two. I can't say he is
and I can't say he ain't..."

Question by assistant DA Richard Burnes:

"Q. You must have some idea about how much taller he
(Bertrand) would be than Clay Shaw.

"A. I see him on TV—He is a tall cat—I don't believe the person
I know as Clay Bertrand is as tall as him. I don't know. I can't say
yes, and I can't say no. As God is my judge. I have to go back to the
same thing I am telling you—I go to a fag wedding reception—and

he is standing up and he is well dressed—I don't measure the guy then, I don't measure him now. I don't even think about the guy. Just like you go to any wedding reception, you mingle, you drink, you talk. I had no occasion to—to have this guy impress me."

And later:

"I get the impression you all want me to identify Clay Shaw as Clay Bertrand. I'll be honest with you that is the impression I get—

"Q. Well?

"A. And I can't. I can't say he is and I can't say he ain't...I cannot say positive, under oath, that he is Clay Bertrand or he is not.

"Even with me listening to the guy's voice on the phone, the voice I recall is somewhat similar to this cat's voice, but his voice has overtones just like Mumu (assistant DA Andrew Sciambra) said, the voice I recall on the phone as Clay Bertrand is a deep, cultured, well-educated voice—he don't talk like me, he used the King's English. Everybody thinks I am holding something back. They think I have the key to who killed Kennedy—I wish I did. I'd sell it and make a million dollars.

More questioning by Burnes:

"Q. Do you know Dave Ferrie?

"A. Yes, I knew Dave Ferrie.

"Q.What were the circumstances of knowing Dave Ferrie?

"A. '54 to '59 I represented Carlos Marcello in his immigration matter and I left his employ in November, October of '63—they shipped him off to Guatemala and he came back from Guatemala and the government had him on trial for something. Dave Ferrie—I met, I think, with Wray Gill and Carlos and they were asking me points in the facets of the Marcello vs. U.S. that I handled in his deportation proceeding.

"Q. Have you ever had any occasion to do any work for Dave Ferrie?

"A. No...

"Q. Had he ever called you in behalf of a client?

"A. No. Wouldn't use him if he did, he ain't the best source in town, you know.

"Q. Has he ever required you to do anything for a subject that might have been arrested?

Dean Adams Andrews Jr., the lawyer convicted of perjury by District Attorney Jim Garrison, grins behind his dark glasses as he answers newsmen's questions.

T

Gesturing like a song-and-dance team, attorneys Sam Monk Zelden, (lef
and Dean Adams And ews Jr. enter the parish courthouse.

Eugene Davis, whom Andrews says is really Clay Bertrand. Davis denies it.

"A. No. No. The only thing I recall doing was recently. I don't know how far back, but he had an expired brake tag ticket—and I used to run a traffic court, but I have been suspended. I don't run it no more—I think I nolle prosequied (sic) the expired brake tag. The reason was the windshield was broken, they put a new windshield on it, something like that, anyway I recall nolle prosequiing the expired brake tag—the car was not his, he had borrowed it from somebody else.

"Q. That was for Dave Ferrie and you dismissed the case?

"A. Right. Declined to prosecute him.

"Q. Did you have occasion to parole anyone for him?

"A. No.

"Q. Do you know what parole power is?

"A. You got to be joking. You ask me an intelligent question and I give you an intelligent answer. Sure I know what it is.

"Q. Will you tell the gentlemen what parole power is?

"A. In Jefferson Parish assistant district attorneys prior to Jan. 1, 1967, were authorized to parole for purposes of making bond persons arrested and incarcerated in jail.

"A. You never paroled anyone for Dave Ferrie?

"A. Not to my knowledge . . ."

(During his trial, Jefferson Parish authorities testified that Andrews paroled a man named Tommy Clark for Dave Ferrie.)

Burnes questioned Andrews as to whether "Bertrand" discussed a fee in the Oswald phone call. Andrews said:

"On a case like that—you better believe it—I would go for nothing—I would become famous."

"Q. Mr. Andrews, didn't you tell us in our office that he said don't worry about a fee?

"A. I don't recall, Dick. You people got me at a disadvantage. You don't know how I work in my office. You don't know how I handle my books and if you ask anybody in town I'm the easiest mark in the world—if you need help I go help.

This wasn't exactly what Andrews had told the Warren Commission. In that testimony, he stated that he would like to see Bertrand again because Bertrand owed him some money. Asked what he would do if he found him, Andrews answered:

"I would beat him with a chain."

More questions by Burnes:

"Q. Now, what was the nature of your being contacted by Clay Bertrand at that time?

"A. You are the only guy in all of them that ever asked me that. I'll elucidate—like in Enrico Caruso.

"Q. You mean you have never been asked why Clay Bertrand contacted you?

"A. That's right. You're the first one who ever asked me.

"Q. How about the Warren Committee?

"A. No, they contacted it in a different way—they got an answer out of me but they never got the whole thing.

"Q. All right, would you tell us...

"A. A voice that I identify as Clay Bertrand called me at the hospital and asked me if I would represent Lee Oswald in Dallas—nobody ever asked me about a fee or anything else—he said I would get real famous and he would get in touch with Lee Oswald so that I could represent him. That's the part nobody ever asked me. As soon as I said I heard the voice of Clay Bertrand, blump! They all cut off. You're the first one who ever asked me for the whole bit. . ."

Burnes asked Andrews if he told anyone about the Bertrand call, and Andrews replied that the first person he told was "Sgt. (Prentiss) Davis, my office man." The next person he told, he said, was Zelden, and this was on Sunday.

Burnes asked Andrews what he told Davis. Andrews replied:

"All I told him was we were going to Dallas to defend Oswald."

"Q. You didn't tell him it was Clay Bertrand?"

"A. Man, I'm the boss—I don't tell my flunkeys all my business. I pay 'em and they do what I tell them to do or they hit the road. I have no confidant with all my people. I run my office, the tail don't wag the dog. . ."

Later, Andrews provided his growing audience with a good reason for laughter when he made a comical move of harassment against Truth and Consequences.

May 19, Andrews called the Louisiana Secretary of State's office in Baton Rouge and reserved by phone the corporate name "Truth and Consequences Inc." for a period of 90 days. He had until August 19 to make a formal charter request. Asked what he planned to do with the name, Andrews said, "Sit on it," then added that he had a client who might make a formal charter request. He said, "An ounce of prevention is worth a pound of cure. Just a defensive measure."

When he was indicted for perjury, Andrews entered a plea of innocence, and Zelden claimed the indictment was not specific enough. The grand jury then reindicted him, citing the testimony related above. There the matter stood until June 12, when Criminal District Judge Frank J. Shea set his trial for Aug. 9.

On June 28, Ed Planer, a news editor for WDSU, the New Orleans NBC outlet, was subpoenaed and testified before the grand jury. No one would say whether Planer was asked who NBC's Bertrand was, but the same day Andrews came forward of his own accord and broke his long refusal to say whether Shaw was or wasn't Bertrand.

Andrews agreed with NBC that Shaw wasn't. He said the "real" Bertrand is a French Quarter bar owner named Eugene C. Davis, whom Andrews was protecting all this time because "he isn't involved in all this." He didn't explain how the connection with Oswald came about if David wasn't "involved." Nobody knows whether Davis is a homosexual or not, but he hardly met the test of being a "prominent" New Orleanian.

Davis, 42, promptly denied ever using the name Bertrand and called Andrews' claims "lies." He said he was questioned by two FBI agents "a day or two after the NBC broadcast." (NBC said it was giving Bertrand's name to the Justice Department.) He said that after the questioning, one of the agents told him they were satisfied he wasn't Bertrand.

Asked why he had witheld Davis' identify as Bertrand for so long, Andrews retreated behind the cover of his hip talk. He said:

"How would you like to have your brains knocked out and be busted down to your toes."

Asked later to explain this, he said he had been speaking "figuratively." He wouldn't say whom he was afraid of or why.

Davis, 5 feet 9 inches tall, 165 pounds with black hair and brown eyes, doesn't look anything like Shaw, who is 6 feet, 5 inches tall.

When Andrews came up for trial, Zelden withdrew from the case, saying he and Andrews could not agree on strategy. Actually, Zelden had little choice in the matter. During the weeks immediately before the trial, Andrews failed to inform Zelden of a number of moves he made in connection with the trial and continuously failed to show up for meetings scheduled with Zelden. Publicly, Zelden said he was withdrawing because he and Andrews couldn't agree on strategy. Andrews' comment to this was: "Aw, he's fulla bull."

Andrews, defending himself, failed on a last minute motion to recuse Garrison as prosecutor claiming the DA had "personal interests" which were not in keeping with the "fair and impartial administration of justice." At the end of that first day in court, August 9, Andrews commented: "Fat man's had a rough day." He continued to have a rough time during the trial itself when he was defended by three brothers, Harry, Cecil and Bruce Burglass.

After five days in court, with Judge Shea driving the case forward until, late each evening, Andrews was convicted on three of five counts of perjury. He has been sentenced to three concurrent terms of 18 months.

Andrews has predicted Garrison's probe will fall flat on its face. He told a States-Item newsman the end would not be long in coming, saying: "I meet these two guys in a bar and I say what are you doing down here cause I know what line of work they're in. They tell me they're keeping a clock on big Jim and when the time comes, they're going to put the hat on the giant. I say ho, ho, ho, what can I do for you?"

Meantime, though, Andrews has been convicted - - a victory for the giant if only in terms of public relations, and a crushing blow for the Fat Man.

Even if Andrews is successful when he appeals his conviction, he's had it professionally. He's lost his job as assistant Jefferson DA, his law practice has dwindled away to nothing, he's broke, with no means of caring for his wife and four children.

He has a bad heart, which no doubt has been aggravated in the last few months.

All in all, a heavy price for receiving one phone call.

Chapter Seven

You Can't Tell The Umpires
Without A Scorecard

'This is a government of laws, not of men."

So reads the stone-graven inscription on the dingy old grey elephant of a building at the traffic-congested intersection of Tulane Avenue and Broad Street in New Orleans. The drabness of the structure is relieved only somewhat by a few Greek columns scattered across the many-stepped front entrance.

The building is as ugly as the reason for the existence of the agencies and institutions housed therein. All of the people there are employed as a result of crime.

Most of them, though, never expected to be in the center of the crime of the century, one of the ugliest crimes of all, the assassination of President Kennedy.

Through most of 1967, public interest in that crime was directed at the happenings behind those dirty stone walls. There, District Attorney Jim Garrison spent his days engrossed in the bits and hunks of information he collected in his effort to prove that the President's death was the culmination of a New Orleans-based conspiracy.

Reporters camped outside the tall, heavy mahogany doors leading to Garrison's office in the hope of finding out more about what and whom the investigation involved.

From time to time, as developments in the case warranted, local newsmen were joined in their vigil by hordes of other journalists from other parts of the country and world.

Garrison's office is located at the dark end of one of the long, high-ceilinged, marble-floored halls and is entered through the polished mahogany doors, which are brightened by large brass letters with back-lighting. The letters spell JIM GARRISON.

The DA's office was the primary target for out-of-town newsmen as they arrived, but the building is important to the news story created by Garrison for reasons other than that his office happens to be there.

As you get to Garrison's office you can't miss seeing the door leading to the room where the Orleans Parish Grand Jury secrets itself during weekly sessions. The grand jury was drawn into the Garrison investigation and returned several indictments in connection with the case.

Clay L. Shaw, the first man to be bound over for trial in the Kennedy assassination, was indicted after a four-day preliminary hearing in March, 1967, on a charge of participating in a conspiracy to murder the President.

Dean Andrews, who first brought the name of the mysterious Clay Bertrand, into the case was indicted by the Jury for perjury, as was Layton Martens, a former roommate of the late David William Ferrie.

The jury questioned other witnesses in connection with the probe and others may be yet to come.

The building also houses, in addition to New Orleans Police Headquarters, the offices of Criminal Sheriff Louis A. Heyd Jr., whose staff has figured in the case through serving subpoenas for Garrison and the grand jury and handling security for the hearings in the case.

But the Criminal District Courts Building, as its name implies, is really the stronghold of eight judges, an august body Garrison once challenged to full-scale war when he called them "sacred cows."

The eight criminal district judges of Orleans Parish became as deeply entangled in Garrison's investigation as Garrison himself as the legal actions began to multiply. Garrison's role was one of accusation and the judges' that of ensuring fair trials for all of the accused.

Of the eight judges on the court at the time that the Kennedy probe here began five were on the bench in the days of Garrison's spectacular feud with the jurists in 1962. The three new judges were all Garrison allies at the time they took the bench, though they subsequently proved less so. They are Judges Frank J. Shea, Matthew S. Braniff and Rudolph F. Becker. All replaced anti-Garrison judges on the bench.

The eight men on the bench during the Kennedy probe are personalities in their own right, apart from their relations with Garrison. Some, like the DA, have in the past been controversial political figures, even to the point of politics-inspired fist fights in one case. And both as a group and as individuals, they have had stormy dealings with Garrison in the past.

Judge Edward A. Haggerty Jr., the judge allotted the trial of the first man ordered to court in the Kennedy case, is a man who had considerable experience in the role of state prosecutor.

He spent 11 years as an assistant DA under five district attorneys before he was elected to the Criminal Court bench in 1956. During those years, he was assigned as prosecutor to some of the hottest local cases. The most famous was the Diddie Wolfolk Cooper murder trial in 1954, which had the local folk chanting "Who did Diddie in?"

He was considered an extremely tough prosecutor and his associates today say he is an astute jurist, a stickler for order and decorum in his courtroom.

Although the judge permits no nonsense in court, the social Haggerty is a jovial, fun-loving, hard-drinking poker player, who doesn't mind if his constituents see him in his cups now and then.

Haggerty, who is stocky and has Irish written all over his face, demonstrates a not-bad tenor with little cajoling. He takes an active role in the annual St. Patrick's Day festivities of New Orleans (which is every bit as much Irish as it is French).

Each year Haggerty can be seen marching in the St. Pat's Day parade through the Irish Channel, the historically Irish section of the city.

Every year, too, the judge is host at a Christmas party in his chambers for his staff and friends at the courthouse, a party which is traditionally concluded by Haggerty's rendition of "Danny Boy."

A native of New Orleans, Haggerty was born in 1913 and graduated from St. Aloysius High school in 1932. He received his law degree from Loyola University in 1940 and two years later was appointed an assistant DA under then district attorney J. Bernard Cocke, later a criminal district judge himself and a hard and bitter foe of Garrison.

Haggerty subsequently served as assistant DA under Leon D. Hubert, Severn T. Darden, Herve Racivitch and James O'Connor.

He left the DA's office in February of 1942 and served with the U.S. Navy for four years, participating in the invasion of Saipan in the South Pacific. He returned to the office in 1946. Haggerty ran for judge in 1956, campaigning for and winning the seat vacated by the retirement of Judge Fred Oser.

Judge Oser was the father of Alvin Oser, who is heavily involved in Garrison's probe as an assistant DA. Another bit of coincidence involving Haggerty is that in the Diddie Cooper case the foreman of the grand jury was Albert V. LaBiche, foreman of the jury which indicted Shaw.

And a final coincidence: Judge Haggerty drew the Shaw trial by chance, and the public alottment was made in the office of his father, clerk of court Edward A. Haggerty Sr.

Like Haggerty, Judges Shea, Braniff, Becker, Oliver P. Schulingkamp, Malcolm V. O'Hara and Thomas M. Brahney Jr. put in years as public prosecutors before ascending to the bench.

Like Haggerty, all are New Orleans natives and Louisiana-educated.

Judge Schulingkamp began law practice in New Orleans in 1946 after four years of Navy service in the Pacific. In 1942, he was appointed assistant U.S. Attorney and placed in charge of the prosecution of cases developed by the FBI. Between 1952 and 1954, he was an assistant DA and between 1954 and 1956 he served as a special assistant to the state Attorney General.

Schulingkamp was defeated in his first campaign for criminal court judge, but in 1960 was appointed by Gov. Earl K. Long to fill out the term of the late Neils F. Hertz Sr. He then won an election to keep his seat.

Judge Shea, 39, is the youngest of the criminal court judges, but not the junior in length of service. He has been an associate counsel for the criminal division of the Legal Aid Bureau for two years when he was named an assistant DA by Leon Hubert in 1957. He held this post for a year and a half.

Shea entered a race for judge of city Traffic Court in 1962, but withdrew. He rejoined the DA's office under Garrison and with Garrison's support ran for criminal judge in 1963. He defeated Guy Johnson, who originally was a defense attorney for Shaw but withdrew in the early stages of the case.

Shea and Garrison are no longer political buddies, reportedly as a result of a quarrel over Shea's brother John, who was fired from his post as assistant DA by Garrison.

Judge Bernard Bagert

Judge Rudolph Becker

Judge Thomas Brahney

Judge Matthew Braniff

Judge Edward Haggerty

Judge Malcolm O'Hara

Judge Oliver Schulingkamp

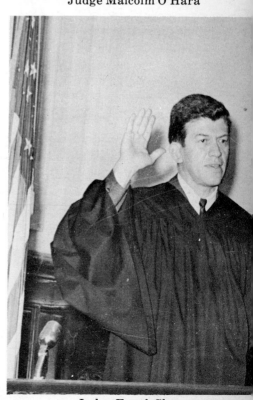

Judge Frank Shea

During the summer of 1966, Shea had a humorous public battle with the city over the lack of air conditioning in his courtroom. He subpoenaed the mayor and city finance director to appear before the grand jury and explain why there was no air conditioning and caused a general stir, resulting in such headlines as "Hot Judge Loses Cool."

Garrison remarked that Shea had as much power to disband the United Nations as he did to use the grand jury to cool off his courtroom.

Shea, like a young schoolmarm having trouble with discipline, manages to preserve the dignity of his courtroom only by concealing a naturally joking, unreserved manner behind a stern voice and unsmiling countenance.

O'Hara was a state senator in 1962 when he formally announced his candidicy to succeed his retiring father, William J. O'Hara, as judge of the Criminal District Court.

The 45-year-old honor graduate of Tulane University Law School was an assistant DA from 1954 through 1956 and first assistant DA through 1958. That year he ran for DA against Richard Dowling (the man Garrison beat four years later.) O'Hara won by a small margin, then was unseated as the Democratic nominee by the state Supreme Court in a 4-3 decision after irregularities in the election were charged. He went on to become an assistant city attorney, then a state senator.

When his father announced his retirement, O'Hara (by then co-floor leader of the Orleans Parish Senate delgation) ran for his father's seat and won. He took office in September of 1962, in the period when Garrison's feud with the judges was heating up.

O'Hara and Garrison had been friends, but O'Hara generally went along with the rest of the judges during their dispute with Garrison. In his 1958 bid for DA, O'Hara had said he would make Garrison his first assistant if he were elected.

Then, in 1965, O'Hara made his final break with Garrison by running against Big Jim as the DA sought a second term in office.

O'Hara was criticized widely for refusing to resign as a judge while campaigning for DA. He took a leave of absence instead, and the elder O'Hara came out of retirement to take the bench while his son fought Garrison.

The campaign, which originally included another former Garrison ally, Frank Klein, was dirty. Klein, who had quit Garrison's office in a dispute over the DA's chief investigator, Pershing Ger-

vais, made Gervais a political target. Gervais was sacrificed and
Klein dropped out of the running.

O'Hara went on television and claimed Garrison had a bad serv-
ie record with regard to his mental health. Garrison retorted he
would send O'Hara to jail for illegal use of a military record, but
didn't press the point.

O'Hara said Garrison was given a medical discharge from the
Army National Guard during the Korean war because he had "an
anxiety reaction." O'Hara produced a photocopy of a document
which he said showed that Garrison's discharge was based on the
reaction, which he described as " the ugly force in him that drives
him to destroy everyone who fail to bow to his will. . .it used to be
called a Napoleonic complex."

Since he became district attorney, O'Hara said, Garrison has
viciously attacked friends who were his supporters and teachers,
judges of the Criminal District Court, the New Orleans Police Department, the newspaper which supported him as a candidate, the
state Legislature, the state Supreme Court and the Criminal
Courts Bar Association.

He said the Garrison administration has been marked by the
"greatest turnover in assistant DA's in the entire history of law
enforcement in New Orleans." He said this was because "decent,
honorable men who served" in Garrison's office "could not stom-
ach" his practices.

O'Hara's remarks were made during the heat of a political campaign, and apparently didn't make a great deal of impression on
the voters. Garrison won two to one. But Garrison's actions — before and since — support O'Hara's point. Many newsmen feel that
Garrison has a McCarthyist streak in him. He reacts violently to
criticism, and often seems to take the attitude that anyone who is
not for him is against him.

As Gov. McKeithen said recently, he hates to criticize Garrison
because "he has a habit of criticizing back."

Garrison said he contracted amoebic dysentery in Europe during World War II, and it recurred during the Korean war. He said
the medical discharge was because of this, and the so-called "anxiety reaction" was based on his physical difficulties. He pointed to
his continued service with the National Guard as evidence that he
was not considered mentally unfit for military service.

O'Hara also claimed Garrison exhibited a "terrible lack of dili-
gence" in his job. Garrison struck back, calling O'Hara a "hired
gun," sent to shoot him down. Garrison won handily and O'Hara

went back to the bench. Leon Hubert, attorney for the Warren Commission, is a law partner of O'Hara.

Another aggressive campaigner, Judge Brahney, stirred the city with his successful race for judge in 1958. He ran for the post against the then DA Hubert, claiming that Hubert hadn't "the courage to warrant promotion to the bench." He accused the then Mayor Chep Morrison (who had defeated Brahney in the 1954 mayor's race) of "tampering with the grand jury" in an investigation concerning the police superintendent. He charged Hubert had failed to take action against the mayor.

Brahney, who received his law degree from Loyola University in 1942, was an assistant U. S. Attorney from 1946 to 1949 and a member of the City Council from 1950 to 1954, but he has generally been as active in civic work as in politics, serving on committees and boards for such organizations as the National Conference of Christians and Jews, the Citizens Advisory Committee on Housing Improvement for the city and the Milne Home for Boys.

Judge Braniff has been jumping into the middle of things with both feet since before World War II. In that conflict, he couldn't wait for the U.S. to get involved. He joined the Canadian Royal Air Force in 1941, later transfering to the U.S. Air Force and serving as a tailgunner throughout the war.

Earlier, after he received his law degree from Loyola in 1937, Braniff joined in organizing the Good Government League and created a sensation by charging that a grand jury had been handpicked to whitewash a tax racket.

On two occasions, Braniff's political disputes reached the point of violence. He was socked on the nose by an unidentified assailant in 1938 in the civil sheriff's office while photographing records with former Gov. James A. Noe.

In 1941, he had a brief, one-punch fistfight with the late Shirley Wimberly, who later also served as a criminal courts judge. Wimberly, supporting Earl K. Long against Noe, landed the punch. Braniff was prominent in many of the old Long vs. Anti-Long factional disputes.

He served as an assistant DA under Herve Racivitch and Severn Darden between 1949 and 1952. While an assistant DA, Braniff clashed with the then Orleans Parish Coroner Dr. C. Grenes Cole when Cole failed to report deaths by criminal abortion to the DA's office. A long investigation and public feud with Cole ensued.

Braniff ran for criminal court judge against incumbent J. Bernard Cocke in 1964. Also in the race was Becker. Braniff lost out in the first primary and threw his support to Becker. Braniff finally became a judge in March, 1966, when he was appointed to succeed the retiring George P. Platt.

Earlier, Becker was elected to the bench in the second primary with the support of Braniff and Garrison over the entrenched incumbent, Cocke. With Garrison directing the campaign and personally writing much of the campaign material, Becker ran on the issue that Cocke was near retirement age and was under the influence of the "old-line political machine." Becker hit hard at Cocke for his tradition of never holding court on Friday, one of the original bones of contention between Garrison and the judges.

Becker took the oath in the presence of Garrison and Becker's son Rudy III, then an assistant DA under Garrison. Garrison said at the ceremony: "Today's swearing in of a new Criminal District Court judge is an auspicious occasion for a number of reasons. Foremost of all, Rudolph Becker is — in the most direct sense — a man elected by the citizens themselves. This should serve as a reminder to all of us that we in public life work for the people. We are not their masters. They are ours. If we fail to do our jobs in the best possible way — or even if the prople merely think we have failed — they have a perfect right to critize us. Their right to comment on our public performance or to replace us if they choose is not merely a privilege — it is the life and very soul of our democracy."

Becker had 37 years of experience in the practice of criminal law before running for judge. Five years of that time was spent as an executive assistant DA.

The only one of the eight judges who was never a public prosecutor is Bernard J. Bagert, 54, who was appointed to the court in 1956 by Gov. Long.

Bagert, who has been a practicing attorney since 1935, got his seat on the bench after being a ward worker in the Seventh Ward for the Regular Democratic Organization, then a potent factor in local politics. He gave up his RDO ties after taking the bench, saying it would be improper for a judge to have this association. Bagert was senior judge of the court at the time of the Garrison probe.

A past district commander of the American Legion, Bagert is known as "Bennie" to his friends, and ordinarily is an affable character. But the short, heavy-set judge is reported to have engaged in a recent scuffle with Lloyd Cobb, head of the International Trade Mart and Clay Shaw's former boss. Cobb is a much bigger man, but Bagert is light on his feet. Bagert won't own up to the ruckus.

By mid-1967, all of the judges had been involved in the Garrison probe in some way. Bagert, O'Hara and Braniff made up the three-judge panel which concluded that Garrison had presented enough evidence at a preliminary hearing to bind Shaw over for trial. Haggerty got the case to try.

Judge Shea presided at the perjury trial of Dean Andrews, and Schulingkamp was to handle a similar proceeding for Layton Martens. Up to mid-1967, Becker and Brahney had handled only more or less routine motions in the case, but were subject to becoming directly involved at any moment because all criminal proceedings arising out of the case will of necessity go before one or the other of the eight judges. Garrison has promised more arrests and convictions.

Thus, at least the legal aspects of the future of Garrison's case rests in the hands of these eight men. However, it may take more than legal decisions finally to decide whether Garrison was right or wrong. He must not only prove his case to the satisfaction of Louisiana law. Garrison's judge will be history.

Chapter Eight

I Spy

One of District Attorney Jim Garrison's most notable characteristics as a public official has been his penchant for making enemies. At various times, he has taken on such adversaries as the eight Criminal Court judges, the police force, the Metropolitian Crime Commission, the Louisiana legislature, and many others. Somehow, it seemed inevitable that he would sooner or later cross swords with that most esoteric of American institutions, the Central Intelligence Agency.

The CIA is the United States' cloak-and-dagger outfit, its answer to James Bond. It operates world wide in its effort to hold up the American end of sleuthing in the Cold War, and its agents often turn up in the most unlikely places — sometimes even in the United States, where, theoretically, the CIA is not supposed to operate.

The CIA has a public relations problem. Like a baseball umpire, when it does its job well, you never notice it. But when it goofs, it makes the front pages. Occasionally, you'll hear an angry cry from Indonesia or Tanzania or Cambodia that the CIA is meddling in that country's internal affairs. Fidel Castro, in particular, likes to rave and rant that the CIA is plotting to depose him. On more than one occasion, he has turned out to be right.

Everybody knows, of course, about the Bay of Pigs. The CIA was held responsible for its planning. That wasn't the end of the Cuban story, says Garrison. The DA intends to prove that international fiasco had a direct bearing on the events in Dallas on November 22, 1963.

Garrison said he would show Oswald was not a Communist at all, but a government informant who aided the anti-Castro Cubans. (Sources in Garrison's office said Oswald may have been trained as an intelligence agent during his Marine days at Atsugi Air Force Base in Japan, a known CIA instruction camp.)

The CIA phase of the investigation begins with another in the long list of strange and unpredictable characters that have turned up in the Garrison case, this one a handsome 29-year-old named Gordon Novel who has a wide array of talents and interests.

Until recently, Novel owned a part interest in a lively night spot in the French Quarter. He also manufactured eavesdropping e-quipment.

Novel during Shaw's preliminary hearing was subpoenaed to appear before the Orleans Parish Grand Jury. A week later he was subpoenaed for the second time and Garrison discovered he had skipped town.

He turned up in Columbus, Ohio, (and also in McLean, Va., which happens to be the location of CIA headquarters, and where he took a lie detector test) criticizing Garrison's probe as a "witch hunt", then disappeared again. A warrant for Novel's arrest was issued seeking his return to New Orleans as a material witness in the investigation. The warrant was issued and bond set at $50,000, March 23. Novel popped up again, calling the probe an enormous fraud and challenging Garrison to take a lie detector test. Then Garrison's office issued a second warrant for Novel's arrest, charging him with a 1961 conspiracy to burglarize a munitions bunker near Houma, La. When he finally was arrested in Ghanna, Ohio, a suburb of Columbus, on April 1, his bond was set by the court there at $10,000. The bond was posted and he was released.

When extradition proceedings bogged down, the Louisiana House of Representatives adopted three resolutions urging the governors of Ohio, Texas and Iowa to speed up the return of witnesses in Garrison's case. The resolutions were aimed at the return of Arcacha, Novel and Mrs. Lillie Mae McMaines (Sandra Moffett).

But the House rejected an effort to appropriate $50,000 to Garrison's office to help defray the cost of his investigation. The attempt was made by Rep. Risley Triche of Assumption Parish, who said he was asking for the funds following discussions with intermediaries of Garrison and that he was concerned about the use of private funds to finance a public investigation (a reference to Truth and Consequences, Inc.). He drew immediate opposition and the attempt was defeated by a 66 to 31 vote.

In another copyrighted exclusive, the *States-Item* revealed that

Novel had told a number of friends he was a CIA operative and would use this role to fight Garrison's accusation that he burglarized a munitions bunker in Houma, La., in 1961. It was on this charge, technically, that Garrison sought his extradition. Novel offered to return and testify in the JFK case if Garrison would grant him immunity from the burglary charges, but the DA said no.

During a news conference which he called in Ohio, Novel said the munitions incident was "the most patriotic burglary in history" before he was silenced by his attorney. He also said cryptically to an interviewer, "I think Garrison will expose some CIA operations in Louisiana." He did not elaborate.

Novel told friends the bunker was a CIA staging point for munitions destined for the Bay of Pigs attack. He was also quoted as saying he operated an advertising agency in New Orleans as a front for CIA communications, and prepared radio commercials with cryptographic messages to alert agents to the invasion date.

Novel also turned up with a card identifying him as a Brigadier General on the staff of Louisiana Gov. John J. McKeithen claimed it was forged, but Novel says the governor gave it to him after Novel aided him in a political campaign.

He is accused of participating in the burglary along with Sergio Arcacha Smith, 44, of Dallas, who was the leader of a militant anti-Castro organization in New Orleans in the early 1960's.

Arcacha, a Cuban exile who left Cuba shortly after Castro took over, has lived in Dallas for more than three years. He moved from New Orleans to Houston, where he was living at the time of the assassination, and then to Dallas. Arcacha is a well-educated man, now employed in the export division of an air-conditioning firm, and the father of five children.

Arcacha's lawyer, Ernest Colvin, Jr., said that his client would be willing to talk to Garrison about his investigation "so long as he doesn't have to go into the lair of Mr. Garrison." Arcacha earlier had said he would talk to Garrison's men but only in the presence of Dallas authorities, which Garrison rejected. Colvin charged that "Garrison is a man who is power mad" and said Arcacha feared for his life if he returned to New Orleans for testimony. Colvin accused Garrison of using "the law like a damn club".

Also in on the burglary, Garrison said, was the late David William Ferrie, another versatile citizen whose name keeps popping up in all sorts of connections. The address of Arcacha's anti-Castro group in New Orleans was the same as that used by Oswald for his abortive Fair Play for Cuba Committee, which was supposed to be a pro-Castro outfit. Novel has told polygraph operators (during a lie detector test he took at his own instigation) and reporters that the Houma munitions burglary was not a burglary at all, but a war materials pickup made at the direction of his CIA contact.

Layton Martens, the 24-year-old former roommate of David Ferrie, was indicted for perjury by the grand jury on the basis of his testimony concerning the same alleged munitions burglary.

Only a brief portion of his testimony before the jury was revealed in the formal charge. In that portion he told the jury he did not recall ever hearing of or meeting Novel, he did not know the purpose of the trip to Houma and that he did not remember Arcacha being on the trip to Houma.

When Martens, who was at the time of his indictment a senior at the University of Southwestern Louisiana majoring in the cello, appeared to post his bond, he denied that he had made false statements to the jury.

The investigation of Oswald's operations in New Orleans have centered somewhat on the fact that he used the address of a Camp Street building which also housed the offices of two avowedly anti-Communist organizations.

One was the Cuban Democratic Revolutionary Front, headed by Arcacha; the other was Guy Banister Associates, led by the stormy onetime FBI official and former assistant superintendent of New Orleans police.

Arcacha's office was closed officially in 1962, almost a year before Oswald lived in New Orleans for the last time. Banister, though, was still operating his detective agency in the same building when Oswald printed the Camp St. address on Fair Play for Cuba handbills he distributed in the New Orleans area. The weathered granite building stands at the corner of Camp Street and Lafayette Street, with entrances on both streets. Oswald and Arcacha both listed their addresses as 544 Camp; Banister's was 531 Lafayette. In late 1962, still another anti-Castro organization, the Crusade to Free Cuba, of which Arcacha was reportedly a member, used the address to receive mail contributions.

The DA's office reportedly has questioned witnesses who reported seeing Oswald, Banister, Arcacha and the late Dave Ferrie together in the building during 1963. A close friend of Banister's told the States-Item that the former FBI agent was involved in a variety of anti-Communist activities in Latin America during the time he had his office on Lafayette Street and that he stored munitions in his office.

Banister, who died of a heart attack in the summer of 1964, was also reported to have worked in cooperation with a U.S. military intelligence office (in a *States-Item* story May 5, 1967.)

While Oswald was handing our Fair Play for Cuba leaflets in front of the old Trade Mart, just a few blocks from the Banister building, during the summer of 1963, an anti-Castro group led by Ferrie was demonstrating on Canal Street, a few blocks from the Trade Mart.

Garrison's probe of CIA-sponsored acitivities by anti-Castro Cubans was reported sparked by reports that some Cuban groups here were angry with Kennedy because he "closed the door" government military aid to them in the summer of 1963.

The mysterious deaths theorists flourished once again when Banister's name started creeping into the investigation talk.

One of Banister's associates in his detective agency was Hugh F. Ward, also reportedly active in anti-Communist activities in the Caribbean.

Ward, like Banister, is dead. He was piloting a private plane which crashed May 23, 1965, near Ciudad Victoria, Mexico. All aboard, including former New Orleans mayor and OAS Ambassador deLesseps ("Chep") Morrison, were killed.

Then, mysteriously, Garrison subpoenaed for questioning Juan Valdes, a Latin playwright who lives in New Orleans. Garrison did not say why he wanted to question Valdes. However, Valdes was the neighbor who called in police when Dr. Mary Stults Sherman was murdered in her New Orleans apartment during the summer of 1964. Dr. Sherman's knife-mutilated body was set afire in her fashionable uptown apartment. Her murder never was solved.

Novel publically denied any CIA connections until May 25, when the States-Item produced a letter which a handwriting expert confirmed was written by Novel and which refers to his connections with a CIA-front organization.

After the letter was revealed, Steve Plotkin, Novel's attorney, confirmed that Novel worked for the CIA in New Orleans in early 1961. Plotkin also confirmed that Novel drafted the penciled letter, which was found in the former French Quarter apartment of Novel.

The letter was for an unidentified "Mr. Weiss" who apparently is a CIA official. Here is the text of the letter:

"Dear Mr. Weiss:

"This letter is to inform you that District (sic) Jim Garrison has subpoenaed myself and an associate to testify before his Grand Jury on matters which may be classified TOP SECRET. Actions of individuals connected with DOUBLE-CHEK CORPORATION in Miami in first quarter of 1961.

"We have no current contact available to inform of this situation. So I took the liberty of writing you direct and apprising you of current situation. Expecting you to forward this through appropriate channels.

"Our connection and activity of that period involves individuals presently...about to be indicted as conspirators in Mr. Garrison's investigation.

"We have temporarily avoided one subpeona not to reveal Double-Chek activities or associate them with this mess. We want out of this thing before Thursday 3/ /67. Our attorneys have been told to expect another subpcona to appear and testify on this matter. The fifth amendment and/or immunity (and) legal tactics will not suffice.

"Mr. Garrison is in possession of *unsworn* portions of this testimony. He is unaware of Double-Chek's involvement in this matter but has strong suspicions. I have been questioned extensivly by local FBI recently as to whether or not I was involved with Double-Check's parent-holding corporation during that time. My reply on five queries was negative. Bureau unaware of Double-Chek association in this matter. Our attorneys and others are in possession of complete sealed files containing all information concerning matter. In the event of our sudden departure, either accidental or otherwise, they are instructed to simultaneously release same for public scrutiny in different areas simultaneously.

"Appropriate counteraction relative to Garrison's inquisition concerning us may best be handled through military chammels vis (a) vis D.I.A. man. Garrison is presently colonel in Louisiana Army National Guard and has ready reserve status. Contact may be had through our attorneys of current record, Plotkin, Alverez, Sapir."

Gilbert Fortier, a handwriting expert, compared the penciled letter with letters written by Novel to his ex-wife and confirmed that it was written by Novel.

The "D.I.A." referred to in the letter is the abbreviation for Defense Intelligence Agency, an organization established by President Kennedy to supervise the CIA after the disastrous Bay of

Pigs. A recent book, *The Invisible Government,* by David Wise and Thomas B. Ross, (copyright 1964, Random House), identified Double-Chek of Miami as a CIA front through which pilots and other persons connected with anti-Castro Cuban operations were recruited.

Although the letter was undated, the sequence of events it relates places its writing sometime in late January or early February.

Plotkin explained that Novel served as an intermediary between the CIA and anti-Castro Cubans in New Orleans and Miami before the April, 1961, Bay of Pigs invasion. But he added that Novel's CIA work had "little or nothing to do with the Bay of Pigs invasion and certainly had absolutely nothing to do with the assassination of President Kennedy."

Novel later told a reporter he had never been an agent or an operative for the CIA, but said that he had acted as a CIA intermediary until June of 1961. Novel said the munitions take from the Houma bunker, referred to in the charge against Novel by Garrison, were picked up and taken to the late Guy Bannister and then later trucked to Miami.

However, Novel was not mentioned on any of the network programs on Garrison.

DeBrueys, Garrison says, was the local FBI liaison contact with anti-Castro Cuban groups in New Orleans. When Oswald went to Dallas, says Garrison, DeBrueys was trasfered there. When Oswald was killed, DeBrueys was transferred back to New Orleans.

He claimed Novel worked as what he termed "chief of security" for Garrison before "his forced departure from New Orleans" but was really serving as a double agent for "a national news medium."

Plotkin said Novel has tapes, photographs and other data which will be released shortly and will "prove beyond any shadow of a doubt that Mr. Garrison's investigation is a fraud and a hoax."

He said Novel has turned the information over to a national news medium and that tape recordings and other matters in Plotkin's possession will be released in case Novel dies.

Plotkin said he did not know whether the letter produced by the *States-Item* was ever actually sent. "Nevertheless," he admitted, "the only comment is that everything in the letter as far as Novel is concerned is actually the truth." He said the purpose of the letter was to inform "the person to whom the letter was addressed . . . of activities going on in Louisiana."

Garrison has charged that Plotkin and other lawyers representing Kennedy-case figures are being paid by the CIA. Plotkin has denied this.

The DA said: "In my considered judgment, Mr. Burton Klein (attorney for Alvin Beaubouef, a former associate of Ferrie) and Stephen Plotkin are lying when they say that the source of the money they are receiving for helping to obstruct our investigation is not the CIA in Washington.

"Obviously, the CIA—which does not have to account to anyone in the world for the manner in which it dissipates its funds—instructs anyone it hires to say that they are working for someone else.

"The CIA clearly considers itself to be above the truth and engages in the lie as an instrument of policy whenever it so chooses. This was the case during the Warren Commission hearings when it concealed from the commission, the American people and the world the fact that men whom it had employed were involved in the assassination of President Kennedy..." Garrison said.

Another aspect of Garrison's feud with the CIA revolved around his efforts to get federal agents to testify. Garrison subpoenaed FBI agent Regis Kennedy and former agent Warren Debrueys, but they were ordered by U.S. Attorney General Ramsey Clark not to testify. The names of both appear frequently on FBI reports made during the Warren Commission investigation. U. S. Attorney Louis Lacour moved to quash the subpoena. A week later, on May 17, Kennedy appeared before the grand jury after being ordered to do so by Criminal District Judge Bernard J. Bagert. He invoked executive privilege and refused to divulge information. Garrison withdrew the subpoena but damned what he called federal obstruction of his probe.

Garrison also indicated he felt CIA pressure was being used to prevent the extradition of Novel, whom he described as a houseguest of the CIA who is in the position of a canary visiting a cat whom he thinks is a friend of his.

On May 21, there was a report, never verified, that Novel was shot, or shot at, in a visit to Nashville. Garrison said this "didn't surprise him."

Novel painted himself into a legal corner by filing a $50 million damage suit against Garrison and the members of Truth and Consequences, claiming that Garrison had deprived him of his civil rights and defamed his character, using money supplied by the T & C members to do so.

Federal District Judge James A. Comiskey (against whose father Garrison years earlier made his first political race) ruled that Novel would have to return to New Orleans and testify in order to press the suit.

Novel, unwilling to leave his Ohio sanctuary, withdrew the suit through his local attorney, Plotkin.

Then, extradition proceedings against Novel were dropped by Ohio July 3, 1967, when a Columbus judge ruled that Louisiana had not filed any legal extradition papers. The judge said that all of the papers had some kind of defect and that Louisiana had not complied with requests to complete the papers.

Garrison was also named in a federal court suit filed May 19, by Dean Adams Andrews Jr., whom he has accused of perjury in another aspect of the case. Andrews sued for $100,000 on grounds that the DA deprived him of his civil rights. It asked that Orleans Parish Coroner, Dr. Nicholas Chetta, Dr. Esmond F. Fatter, Grand Jury foreman; Albert LaBiche, and DA aides, William Gurvich and Lynn Loisel be subpoenaed.

Yet another blow at Garrison was struck by *Newsweek* magazine in its May 15, 1967, issue which charged that Loisel offered Alvin Beauboeuf a $3,000 bribe and the promise of a job if he would testify in such a way as to help the DA's office establish the alleged plot against Kennedy. According to the magazine Beauboeuf would testify to certain things Ferrie told him about Clay L. Shaw. The article written by Hugh Aynesworth, a Texas newsman who has covered the Kennedy case since the assassination, continued.

"When the DA's men learned that the meeting (at which the offer was made) had been recorded on tape, Loisel and a colleague returned to threaten Beauboeuf. He was told if he got in the way he would be shot. They hauled him down to the courthouse and made him sign a statement that said, in effect, that he didn't consider the offer of $3,000 and a job as a bribe. They told him bluntly that they had enough on him to ruin him."

Aynesworth concluded that "the real question in New Orleans is no longer whether Garrison has 'solved' the assassination. The question is how long the people of the city and the nation's press will allow this travesty of justice to continue."

Garrison's only comment was that the *Newsweek* article was "unworthy of comment."

Many of those who take a dim view of Garrison's activities say he escalated his attacks against the CIA to divert attention from

T-P Photo

This building at 544 Camp Street in New Orleans housed the detective agency of Guy Banister and the headquarters of Sergio Arcacha Smith's anti-Castro organization. It was also the address given by Lee Harvey Oswald for his Fair Play for Cuba group.

T-P Photo

T-F

The late Guy Banister, a former New Orleans police official, and detective agency owner.

Sergio Arcacha Smith, forr New Orleans anti-Castro leader, li in Dallas.

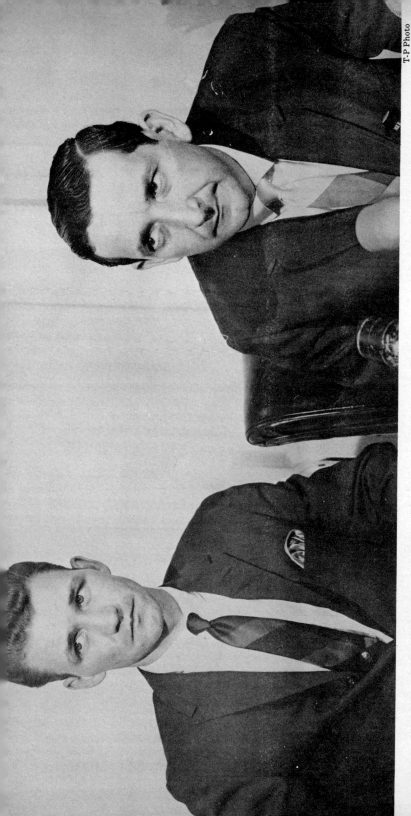

Alvin Beauboef, left, is shown with his attorney, Burton Klein, at a news conference in which they claimed that aides of District Attorney Jim Garrison threatened and attempted to bribe Beauboef to testify against Clay L. Shaw.

T-P Photo

FBI agent Regis Kennedy appeared under court order for questioning in the probe but declined to give information.

New Orleans attorney Steven Plotkin, attorney for Gordon Novel, says his client was associated with the CIA.

Gordon Novel whom Garrison accu of being a CIA agent fled New Orle in March, 1967.

T-P Photo

the bad publicity in *Newsweek* and the earlier article in the *Saturday Evening Post* which cast doubt on the testimony of Perry Raymond Russo.

Late in May, after Garrison made his CIA allegations, Judge Haggerty stiffened guidelines for actions by persons involved in the trial of Shaw and hinted that some persons might be cited for contempt.

Haggerty called a press conference May 29 and said that the reason for the conference was that he felt some had been guilty of contempt.

The judge said that is court "is not trying the Warren Commission report, the FBI, the CIA, the Secret Service or any other agency.

"This court would be less than honest were it not to admit that said agencies may or may not be directly or indirectly related to the trial of Mr. Clay L. Shaw. Such being the case, the widespread comments and charges, directly or indirectly, by persons necessarily involves the future trial of the above entitled case," Haggerty said.

He said he would save his contempt citations for after the trial because they could "bring out all sorts of angles which would further endanger" a fair trial for Shaw.

Haggerty repeated his warnings about contempt citations after NBC broadcast its one-hour special attacking Garrison. Garrison complained that the NBC show was part of an organized attempt by what he calls the "Eastern Establishment" to wreck his case. He sent a formal letter of complaint to the Federal Communications Commission, charging that NBC's Walter Sheridan had harrassed witnesses.

Later, he formally charged Sheridan with public bribery.

The NBC show was followed by four one-hour shows televised by the Columbia Broadcasting System. CBS dealt primarily with questions raised by critics of the Warren Commission, who say shots were fired by more than one person in Dallas. CBS narrator Walter Cronkite did refer to the Garrison investigation but remained more within the guidelines of the court than did NBC. CBS said that it could not draw any conclusions about the validity of Garrison's investigation or any evidence he might have, but the way in which Garrison has handled the probe was criticized.

The network concluded, after conducting its own investigation, that the Warren Report came up with most of the right answers to questions surrounding the assassination. CBS did, however, leave open the possibility that Oswald had been a government agent and the Warren Commission was criticized for not investigating this area more fully.

Shaw and his attorneys denied any CIA connections, but the attorneys admitted Shaw was a director of World Trade Center Corp.

As spring wore on into summer and the probe neared the six-months-old mark, weary newsmen were wondering whether Garrison really meant it when he said the affair might last 30 years. (A statement he later retracted.) But developments continued to pop, the trials of Shaw, Andrews, Martens and the various civil suits filed in the case loomed on the calendar.

And the same questions people the world over have been asking since February 17, 1967 was still on everyone's lips: "What has Garrison got?

Chapter Nine

Plot Or Politics?

At some point, an investigation of the slaying of a President must go beyond the question of who said what to whom at a party in someone's apartment.

A murder case must have a corpus delicti—the body of the crime. This must include a perpetrator, a victim, a motive—in short, a credible set of circumstances.

Anyone who tries to fit the weird succession of events in Dallas in November of 1963 into a logical set of conclusions has his work cut out.

But the Warren Commission, in its own way, did this. Its interpretation of the tragedy is well known. Its findings can be called the lone assassin or "shot in the dark" theory. While to some it might seem unlikely that one semi-crazy Communist could sit in a window high above a passing parade and murder the President of the United States with a couple of lucky shots, even the commission's severest critics must admit that this *possibility* exists and cannot be ruled out without solid evidence to the contrary.

The commission put forward as the lone assassin Oswald and his motive as a dedication to Marxism and, perhaps, a desire to do something to make people notice him. Oswald's almost immediate murder, through a bullet from the gun of Jack Ruby, prevented him from defending himself. Ruby's motive, in turn, was patriotism and anger over the murder of President Kennedy, he said at his trial.

The movements of both men, the Warren Commission said, and the pattern of these movements—in particular Oswald's job in the book depository and Ruby's familiarity with the Dallas police station—made the theory hang together. It was, at least, possible.

The findings of the commission, however, left many unsatisfied and the commission's critics became legion and vocal. The critics squeezed every possible contradiction, every possible doubt out of the 26-volume report and screamed them to the heavens. They also sold a lot of newspapers and books. The key weakness in all of these critics' cases, though, was that they asked a lot of questions they themselves apparently could not answer.

If the Warren Commission was wrong (also at least a possibility), what the devil did happen that day in Dallas and why?

When District Attorney Garrison's probe became public knowledge, the hope was expressed in many quarters that here perhaps was a critic with the investigative authority to produce the truth — or at least a live alternative to the Warren Report.

But, almost immediately, in other quarters the opinion was expressed that Garrison had nothing and that the whole investigation, including an intentional news leak, was aimed at nothing more high-minded than a furtherance of Garrison's own political career. One of the Criminal Court judges complained to Rosemary the day the story of the DA's investigation broke in the-*States-Item* that reporters had "played right into his (Garrison's) hands." The judge said; "You did just what he wanted you to do. You've given him a news break that will splash his name all over and an out at the same time.

"Now, if he's a flop, he'll have had all sorts of national publicity, and he can say his investigation was ruined because the newspaper made it public, and people will sympathize and believe. He can't lose. You all sure are stupid."

Similar feelings were voiced by other New Orleanians and by some newsmen who came tearing into town and read up on Garrison's past history of politicking.

Suddenly, the important question of whether Garrison could rewrite a chapter in recent American history became overshadowed by the question of what Garrison hoped to gain by reopening the investigation of President Kennedy's murder. People were spending as much time talking about Garrison's motivations as they were about what he hoped to prove — a New Orleans-based conspiracy to murder the President.

The question became one of plot, or politics?

The reaction was due partially to the behavior of Garrison himself (who has always been controversial), partially to the writings of persons who believed the Warren Report correct to the Nth degree, partially due to doubts created by the arrest of a man of the stature of Clay Shaw, partially by a typically American distaste for conspiracies.

"He is seeking a Senate seat."

"He thinks he will be the vice-presidential nominee."

"He wants to be governor."

None of these speculations are outside the realm of possibility. Garrison might want to be any one or all three in turn.

To assume that grabbing one of these posts through widespread national exposure was his motive in starting the Kennedy probe, however, seems unlikely and even unfair.

If Garrison wanted to get his name broadcast around the world without really solving the case, he didn't act like it.

He had several outs early in the game.

As the judge said, he could have reaped national exposure then said the newspaper had spoiled his investigation.

When Ferrie died, he could have said, if he really wanted to get out gracefully, that his central witness was dead and he could not proceed.

He could, in view of the developments, have even taken the out that the CIA and the FBI were blocking his every move and that he was forced to give up his quest for the "truth".

Instead, he charged ahead in the locally well-known Garrison manner — stepping on people's feelings (and, perhaps, their rights) making an arrest and allegations that cut off all hope of making a graceful escape from public indignation should he prove to be the fraud some have charged.

Garrison, three times in a row, belittled WDSU — TV(NBC affilliate in New Orleans) reporter Jim Mitchie before his own cameras. Mitchie, a scrappy guy with the guts to ask the questions he wants answered, was accused by Garrison of getting his "stupid" questions from a "switchboard operator", and of being a "birdbrain".

The incident was typically "Garrison" in that his own political ambitions, whatever they are, have never been strong enough to keep him tactful.

Garrison's allegations of "cover-up" by the CIA and other federal agencies were punctuated with demands for a Congressional investigation of the CIA, leading many people to theorize that the DA's investigation was a CIA "witch hunt", with the destruction of that agency the goal in mind.

The most likely explanation of Garrison's motives is that he got interested in what he considered inconsistencies in the Warren Report and that the interest blotted out all other interests.

He has exhibited a habit in the past of driving down one road until he either reaches a dead end or gets bored with the scenery. When he got on the assassination road, the investigation developed out of his curiosity and the scenery has continued to be colorful. If Garrison's motivation is not politics, then, does Garrison believe there was a plot?

It seems clear that when Garrison first got interested he was just checking out the possibility that someone locally might have influenced Oswald to fire the fatal shot in Dallas. It also seems apparent that, when his investigation was first revealed, he had developed a plot theory but had not developed enough solid evidence to back it up in court. Trying to uncover clues about what Garrison was out to prove was difficult at first. The answers were slow in coming.

Garrison, in the beginning, gave out some cryptic hints, but failed to give any specifics for several reasons — anger at being put on the spot, fear that some people he wanted to investigate might get the message prematurely. Too, he probably had not yet filled in the blanks in what was to become his theory about the assassination. Gradually, though, bits and pieces began to bob to the surface and, by early summer, a pattern had emerged that can be called the Garrison theory.

Persistence on the part of newsmen brought it out. After a story appeared in the *States-Item* April 25, 1967, Garrison acknowledged that it contained "essentially correct" information, then proceeded to fill in some of the gaps himself.

The Kennedy plot as seen by the DA revolves around the destruction of hope for a grand Cuban adventure to topple Castro.

Even before the Kennedy administration took office, it was becoming increasingly clear that the Cuban revolution headed by Fidel Castro was becoming Communist-oriented to the point of a Red takeover. The Eisenhower administration in its waning days had severed U.S. relations with the Castro regime, and a host of exiles began flocking to North American shores. The majority of them congregated in Miami, but New Orleans also developed a large Cuban community.

The exiles, bitter at having to leave their homes because of the Communist activity, tended to be what (in the American context) seemed anti-Red extremists, as well they might be. The U.S. government, having its own bone to pick with Castro, sought to direct this enthusiasm toward what it considered a constructive goal — getting rid of Fidel. This led to the disastrous Bay of Pigs invasion of Cuba in 1961, a grievous experience for both the new President and the Cuban exiles.

The exiles felt they had been betrayed. The promised air cover had not come. Their comrades were dead or in prison and in danger of being shot. They were bewildered. Why had their valor been wasted?

The implication to the Cubans of the Bay of Pigs tragedy was that the Brigade had been sacrificed by the United States in the interest of cementing relations elsewhere. The Cuban exiles, though, overcame their bitterness with the realization that America was still their only hope. Robert Kennedy's efforts to free those taken prisoner in the invasion action helped them to swallow their grief.

Then, in the fall of 1962, the exiles got another taste of gall. The missile crisis was in their eyes the perfect opportunity, the perfect excuse, for the United States to forcefully intervene and restore them to their homeland.

The second invasion did not come. Instead, Kennedy, in the fall of 1962, formulated and announced his detente with the Soviet Union.

The exile leaders denounced the action, but they found new hope when Kennedy went to Miami and addressed thousands of them in the Orange Bowl. He promised them they would be back in their homeland free.

In the meantime, Garrison believes, the government had been supplying the Cubans here with the false hope of a second Cuban invasion by sponsoring clandestine training camps.

In New Orleans, the Cuban exiles that fall had support in their demands for a stronger policy toward Cuba. A group of U. S. citizens, known as the Citizens for A Free Cuba, organized to urge stronger U. S. action in connection with the Cuban situation and an implementation of the Monroe Doctrine. Its leaders included Ross Buckley, Cuthbert Brady and Arnesto J. Rogriguez. Other Americans involved in helping anti-Castro organizations included William Dalzell, William Klein, Grady Durham.

Dalzell, Klein and Durham helped to incorporate a couple of anti-Castro Cuban organizations.

Then, there was Guy Banister, who worked closely with Sergio

Arcacha, leader of the local Cuban Democratic Revolutionary front.

And David W. Ferrie, who wanted to fight with them, perhaps out of emotional involvement, perhaps for money.

There were others in New Orleans who helped the exiles merely by contributing their money to the movement for a free Cuba.

The hope was alive.

Kennedy, Garrison believes, cut off this hope during the summer of 1963 by wiping out the training camps, confiscating the caches of war materials and putting an end to hit and run raids on Cuba.

"No legitimate Cuban organization was involved," Garrison says. He describes the persons involved in the plot as "Cuban adventurers" but says that all were not necessarily Cuban in nationality. "There was a mixture of individuals, but the point is they were all anti-Castro oriented and had been engaged in anti-Castro training."

The Kennedy detente, he says, aroused "a vehement reaction from a number of individuals commited to an adventure in Cuba."

Even among the legitimate Cuban organizations through there were strong signs of dissatisfaction backing up this part of Garrison's motive theory. In April of 1963, Dr. Jose Miro Cardona stepped down as the leader of Cubans in exile, charging that President Kennedy had given Fidel Castro "absolute immunity in the execution of Khrushchev's sinister designs."

In a resignation move that split the Cuban Revolutionary Council apart, Miro accused Kennedy of backing out on a promise of a second invasion and of "liquidating" the struggle for Cuba.

Miro, first prime minister of the Castro regime (who later defected) said that Kennedy told him at a meeting in the White House April 10, 1962, nearly a year after the first invasion, that the problem of Cuba was essentially a military one and that the council should contribute the major contingent of soldiers.

"I left the White House with the assurance that the liberation of Cuba would follow soon with Cubans at the vanguard in battle."

He indicated that this was to have been in connection with the Cuban blockade that President Kennedy proclaimed October 22, 1962. Later, he said, U.S. policy on Cuba "shifted suddenly, violently and unexpectedly" and "the struggle for Cuba was in the process of being liquidated by the government."

During the negotiations that followed the blockade, he asserted, Khrushchev maintained his attack and subversion base in the Caribbean, strengthened Castro's military capacity to the point where he could smash an uprising of the Cuban people, and "immobilized" the United States and the rest of the Western Hemisphere.

"The repeated assurances, the constantly renewed promises have been suddenly liquidated," Miro said.

In New Orleans during the same month, Carlos Bringuier of New Orleans, delegate to the Cuban Student Directorate, said his group would continue efforts to liberate Cuba despite action by the U.S. to stop raids originating from U. S. soil.

In May of 1963, the Cuban Committee of Liberation was formed in Miami by Cuban exiles to "wage war on Castro." In an Associated Press story from Miami May 20, 1963, the group was described as reportedly having "the approval of the U. S. government."

This announcement followed a story from Miami May 10 which said: "A new all-out drive to unify Cuban refugees into a single, powerful organization to topple the Fidel Castro regime was disclosed today by exile sources. The plan calls for formation of a junta in exile to mount a three-pronged thrust consisting of sabotage, infiltration and ultimate invasion. The exile sources said the plan had been discussed with Cuban leaders by U. S. Central Intelligence agents. Seeking to put together the junta was Enrique Ruiz Williams, a Bay of Pigs invasion veteran and friend of U. S. Attorney General Robert F. Kennedy. Cuban leaders said intensive sabotage and guerilla activities inside Cuba might start in a month to spark a possible uprising.

"Hundreds of exiles, reported itching for action and resentful of U.S.-imposed curbs against the anti-Castro raids will be recruited to infiltrate Cuba, the sources added."

Then, on June 21, 1963, the Cuban Revolutionary Council said it would demand "the promised help of the United States" if Russian troops attack commandos the council claimed to have landed in Cuba. The council announced only the day before that heavily armed commando forces had been sneaked into Cuba to strengthen the underground in the "first major step of a war of liberation." Antonio de Varona, who had taken over the council after Miro resigned, told newsmen that, "The United States has said publicly that it would help if Russians tried to put down a revolt of the Cuban people. If our troops are attacked by Soviet soldiers, we will demand this help."

Jesse Co

District attorney Jim Garrison has always made news, even when he puts up a campaign bill board. These signs (which did not indicate the office for which Garrison is going to run) encouraged specualtion about his political ambitions.

New Orleans business man Clay L. Shaw, shown here with his attorney, Edward Wegmann (left) and Louis Ivon of the District Attorney's office (right) on the day of his arrest. Garrison charged Shaw with participating in a conspiracy to murder President Kennedy. Shaw is the only person to date who is to be tried for participation in the assassination.

William Gurvitch, Garrison's one-time chief investigator on the Kennedy probe, who resigned from the investigation and urged the Grand Jury to dismiss the charges against Shaw.

These were the public comments of the legitimate Cuban organizations preceding the long,steamy summer of 1963.

During this period the training camps were instituted in various locales, including the New Orleans area.

Two groups, according to the *States-Item* story of May 5, were being trained here for operations against Castro as late as June of 1963. One group was described as being "overt", the other as "covert". One group, reportedly led by Ferrie, was instructed in guerilla warfare employing four to five man teams for infiltration purposes. The training was at a camp in St. Tammany Parish (county) near Lacombe, La., a few miles outside of metropolitan New Orleans. On July 31, 1963, a team of FBI agents raided a summer cottage close to the reported training site and confiscated a ton of war materials, which included 100-pound bomb casings, powder, blasting caps and primer cord. No arrests were made, according to the story. Immediately after the Lacombe raid, the so-called "overt" Cuban troop was disbanded and the men returned to Miami. The "covert" group also slipped out of sight. The *States-Item* story said that on the day following the Lacombe raid, Secretary of State Dean Rusk was conferring with then Soviet Premier Nikita Khrushchev on a proposed nuclear disarmament treaty, and anti-Communist Cubans here reportedly were disturbed over what appeared to them to be a growing rapproachement with the Russians.

The activists were learning guerilla warfare tactics, of a sophisticated nature; they were gearing up, physically and, most important, emotionally.

The less militant were raising funds and getting public support in their efforts.

Meantime, stores of war materials were being collected and stored for the grand adventure. When the training program was disbanded timehung heavy.

The motive for the Kennedy murder then, in the Garrison theory, is bitter disillusionment, a final sense of betrayal.

As one New Orleans Cuban said "You must remember Miami, patron. The big stadium and the speech Mister Kennedy made. He held up the flag and said to us . . . he promised us . . . it was so much of a promise . . . The first of the Bay of Pigs prisoners were there. There had been much bitterness and bad feeling. But it was allowed to pass because he promised us we would go back and be free, and we believed in him. If it began, it began then . . . then with the promise . . . with the hope that could be no hope because the time for hope was already over."

And, if the hope was over for most Cuban exiles, the action was over for the adventurers. Did a small group of the more extreme of the extremists then conclude that their only salvation was a quick change in the American Presidency? And that this hope would be enhanced if the American public believed its beloved President had been murdered by a pro-Castro communist?

Garrison's theory of motive hangs on an affirmative answer to these questions.

The other elements of his assassination theory are concerned with the events:

— Oswald was a scapegoat. He was used only as long as he was needed and then shot.

— The plot was hatched during mid-September in New Orleans.

— Jack Ruby became involved with the group via a gun-running, people-smuggling operation between the Gulf Coast and Cuba.

— All of the men involved were known to federal authorities because at one time or another they had all been employed by federal agencies or involved in activities sponsored by government agencies, namely the CIA and later the FBI.

— The conspiracy was covered up after the assassination when the facts pointed in the direction of some men who had been in the employ of the government.

— Not all of the people involved in the conspiracy, or having knowledge of it, were in Dallas.

— The President was killed by a fatal bullet fired from the front. The events in Dallas, as Garrison sees them, are as follows:

"He was hit from the front. There was a crossfire situation set up, which involved at least two pairs of men in the front — apparently two behind the stone wall and two behind the picket fence, which is a little bit in back of the stone wall.

"The role of the second man in each case was to pick up the actual cartridges, taken on the bounce, so to speak, so that the cartridges could be disposed of as quickly as the guns, which were apparently tossed in the back of cars. There were cars parked immediately behind.

"In addition to those men in front, they had at least one man in the back who was shooting, although it is becoming increasingly apparent that he was not shooting from the sixth floor of the book depository.

"We have located one other person who was involved in the operation. He was one of the adventurers who was involved in the anti-Castro activities, who was not using a gun, but who was engaged in a row in Dealey Plaza in order to aid those who had guns.

"You had in effect a group of men operating as a guerilla team. It was a precision operation, and was carried out very coolly and with a lot of coordination.

"It appears they used frangible bullets. They are forbidden by the Geneva Treaty, but are the kind of bullets that are quite often used — or would be used — for an assassination project by intelligence forces or forces employed by an intelligence agency, because there is assurance even beforehand that there will be no bullets, no slugs remaining, with any of the landmarks of the guns to help authorities identify the guns. Frangible bullets explode into little pieces."

Garrison, referring to the bullet found at Parkland Hospital in Dallas, said, "It was dropped on one of the cots at the hospital." The Warren Report said the bullet in question passed through President Kennedy and struck Texas Gov. John Connally.

A close reading of the testimony in the 27-volume Warren Report relating to the events in Dealey Plaza and the medical and ballistics tests leave the authors with these conclusions:

1. There is ample testimony to support theories other than the conclusions reached by the Warren Commission.

2. There is ample evidence to cast doubt on the opinions expressed by Garrison as to how the assassination took place.

3. If the same standards of criticsm are applied to the Warren Commission's conclusions as to Garrison's statements, there is ample room for doubt there, too.

Garrison, of course, is not bound by what is presented in the report. He says he has other evidence, which he cannot reveal until the trial of Shaw.

He has never said specifically whether he believes Oswald stood at the sixth floor window of the Texas Book Depository building as a decoy and did not fire, or if someone else fired from the window. But three witnesses thought they saw a gun fired from the window, and it would not have been easy for an individual not connected with the depository to have gotten in, done the shooting and escaped without being seen.

Testimony before the commission shows a wide difference of opinion as to the source of the shots. In fact, more of those who testified thought they came from the direction of the grassy knoll than from the book depository. (shots from the knoll, down the street from the depository, would have struck the President from the right or front, rather than from the rear.) Trained observers such as secret servicemen and law officers said they heard shots from the knoll. Lawmen converged on the knoll after the shooting in the belief that the shots came from there.

Several witnesses said they saw people fleeing from the knoll. Two saw puffs of smoke amid the trees atop the knoll. Police found no one there, but did find tracks — leading in opposite directions. There was a mass of cars parked behind the knoll, and this is apparently where Garrison feels the guns were stashed.

This "evidence" does not go very far toward establishing Garrison's contention that the shots came from the knoll, but on the other hand a close examination of the testimony from which the commission concluded they came from the window leads you into some pretty tough problems.

It is beyond the scope of this book to analyze the Warren Report except insofar as it relates directly to Garrison's investigation. But other writers have extensively documented this point — the source of the shots — as the report's weakest link. It involves shooting technique probably far beyond Oswald's ability, a highly improbable "delayed reaction" by Gov. Connally to the shot which hit him, and an incredible performance on the part of the "magic bullet" which is said to have gone all the way through both Kennedy and Connally while losing less metallic weight than was left in Connally's wounds!

The most damaging testimony to Garrison is the ballistics report showing the two bullet fragments found in the Presidential car were fired from Oswald's rifle to the exclusion of all others. A source close to Garrison says the DA believes the FBI falsified this part of the report.

The sum of the testimony indicates to the authors that in order to accept either Garrison's or the Commission's version of the events in Dallas, it is necessary to ignore or impeach a goodly amount of expert and eyewitness testimony.

These are the elements of the DA's theory.

Garrison offers a motive, a possible set of perpetrators, an explanation of what he thinks happened in Dallas in November of 1963.

It is up to you to decide whether they are a credible set of circumstances. It is up to Garrison to prove they are not only credible, but actual.

One of the attractive aspects of the lone assassin conclusion was that it obviated the necessity of accounting for any killers still on the loose. Conversely, one of the difficulties of a conspiracy theory is that it assumes a plot so well-conceived and executed that it eluded the combined efforts of the Secret Service, the FBI, the Warren Commission and everybody else.

The Garrison theory takes this bull directly by the horns. Let us suppose the CIA did employ some less than reliable characters.

Let us suppose that on that unhappy day in November, 1963, that organization's high officials found that persons once employed by them were deeply involved in the President's demise. What then?

Is it not possible to guess (without sounding too much like a New Leftist, or like *Ramparts* magazine) that the American Establishment would rally to supress this information? Could not then the vast investigative powers of the CIA and FBI be turned toward burying the evidence, rather than uncovering it?

Tom Bethell, a London schoolteacher who came to New Orleans to study jazz and somehow wound up on Garrison's investigative staff, reported July 1 the CIA has concealed at least 51 official document vital to the probe.

Bethell, researching the National Archives in Washington, said the list of concealed information shows the CIA "knew a great deal" about Oswald before the assassination.

The documents are labeled "S" for secret or "TS" for top secret and only the titles are available to the public. Some are not labeled but are considered classified anyway.

The documents are among 1,555 Warren Commission documents in the archives. Of the total, about 1,200 are unclassified and available to the public.

Among the available documents, Bethell said, is a notarized statement by State Department officer J. D. Crowley, saying "The first time I remember learning of Oswald's existence was when I received copies of a telegraphic message dated Oct. 10, 1963, from the CIA, which contained information pretraining to his current activities."

You can take Garrison's line of reasoning or leave it, but his theory does offer a handy explanation of why certain obstacles have been placed in the path of persons trying to dig out facts about the Kennedy assassination, including Garrison. It also fits in with the theories of the Warren Commission's critics, such as Mark Lane, who argue that the commission considered only evidence that tended to support its one-assassin theory.

One is not, of course, forced to choose exclusively between what is now the Garrison theory and the Warren Report. There are other theories being touted right now, one of which is that Kennedy was the victim of a plot instigated and executed by organized crime. This theory offers a believable set of perpetrators and a possible motive. No evidence has been offered, however.

All right, you might well say, the box score on evidence now stands at: Warren Report, 27 volumes. Organized crime theory, zero. Garrison theory???

Most of what Garrison has made public in the way of evidence consists of the highly suspect testimony of two individuals, Perry Raymond Russo and Vernon Bundy, the former elicited under hypnosis and the other based on what a man says he saw just before he plunged a needle into his arm for one of his habitual heroin fixes. All they said was they saw a man they identified as Clay Shaw. Russo said he overheard a conspiracy being hatched with Shaw in on it. Bundy says he saw Shaw with Oswald.

(The Defense is expected to spring its own mystery witness that may further discredit Russo's testimony.)

Garrison also produced the notation of "P.O. 19106" from Clay Shaw's address book and said it was the same as a number in Oswald's notebook. The P.O. 19106 in Oswald's book had no identification. The number in Shaw's book carried the notation, Lee Odom, Dallas, Tex.

Garrison said the number in coded form was the unpublished 1963 telephone number of Jack Ruby. Lee Odom turned up in Irving, Tex., though, and said he had had that post office box number for about three months in 1966 only and that he had met Clay Shaw in New Orleans in 1966 when he came over to try to promote a bull fight. The Post Office says this box number did not come into existence until 1965.

If there's any more evidence that would implicate Shaw, Garrison hasn't talked of it, in keeping with the guidelines set down by the court.

Shaw was only charged with participating in a conspiracy.

What about the other elements of the Garrison theory?

The case is cluttered with a bevy of Cubans he has questioned or whose names have been mentioned in connection with the investigation.

At this writing he has not arrested a single Cuban. Some are being questioned simply for information; others are actively aiding Garrison in his investigation; the connection of still others is, at this point, hazy.

The relation of Oswald to any of these people is not well-established, particularly in view of the conflicting descriptions of his appearance. Garrison has not explained how Oswald happened to become the "patsy" of the conspirators.

What he must yet produce is one piece of solid evidence that places a group of New Orleans-based adventurers in Dallas with guns in their hands on the parade route November 22, 1963 — evidence that will stand the toughest kind of cross examination in court.

There is much to make one skepical about Garrison's case. Sometimes, you are forced to rub your eyes and ask if there really is a Garrison.

It would seem incredible that Garrison would risk destroying himself on a quixotic venture unless he had some confidence in the outcome, and he exudes self-confidence.

It would seem incredible, that is, if the DA is in his right mind. Could it be that this highly intelligent man, never the stable sort, has been lured by this case into a maze of mental convolutions that has finally alienated him from reality? It's a theory that was being subscribed to in some quarters.

The flaw in this argument is that Garrison is surrounded by a reasonably able and sane set of aides who have careers and ambitions of their own. If those close to the situation see that he is embarked on a disaster course, it is reasonable to ask why none have defected.

None of Garrison's assistant DA's have deserted since the probe became public, but he did spectacularly lose a man who had publicly been termed his chief investigator in the Kennedy probe.

William Gurvich, head of a private detective agency, was a prominent figure in the probe up through Shaw's preliminary hearing and after. Suddenly, on June 22, it was reported that he had met with U.S. Sen. Robert F. Kennedy of New York, the late President's brother, and told him the Garrison probe was a "hoax". Gurvich said later he did not call the probe a hoax, saying "it's one thing to call it a hoax and another to say there's nothing to it."

Gurvich returned to New Orleans and went before the grand jury in an effort to get the charges against Shaw dismissed. The jury heard him and did not act.

He made a number of charges against Garrison, including claims that the DA planned to have the local FBI office raided and that before David William Ferrie's death he wanted to kidnap Ferrie and torture him by tearing off his false hair. (Those who know Garrison are accustomed to hearing him make outrageous statements. Nobody takes them seriously.)

Gurvich said there was no basis for the charges against Shaw or for the probe in general. (He had told *States-Item* reporters the exact opposite only a few weeks earlier.)

A spokesman for Garrison said Gurvich was never a part of the DA's regular staff but was brought into the assassination probe for special purposes such as photography. The spokesman added that guidelines set down by Judge Edward Haggerty Jr. for principals in the Shaw case prevented any further comment.

Gurvich made some serious charges relating to Garrison's mental condition, which the local press did not carry. The authors, who have known Garrison for some time, make no judgement but present the theory as one put forward by some observers of the case. Again, it must be pointed out that none of Garrison's regular aides have deserted him.

Where does this leave us? Was there a conspiracy? Or is the Warren Commission correct in its conclusions?

Certainly, not enough evidence has been produced to rule out the possibility that the Warren Report is correct, or nearly so.

The Warren Report's answers are not strong enough, on the other hand, to have satisfied everyone's doubts.

As Garrison says, "John F. Kennedy was President of all of us, and the truth about his death belongs to all of us."

The truth, whatever it may be, is important and there has been a strange, almost ominous reluctance on the part of constituted authorities other than Garrison to delve further than the closed book of the Warren Commission's investigation.

Garrison might be dead wrong. However, he is the only public official with investigative power actively pursuing an inquiry into the assassination. History deserves a better break than that.

Appendix

Alphabetical Listing of all persons connected with the probe of the Kennedy assassination by the office of the District Attorney of Orleans Parish.

JAMES C. ALCOCK, an assistant district attorney heavily involved in Garrison's assassination investigation, is probably the best courtroom lawyer in Garrison's office.

GILBERTO ALVAREDO, probably a Mexican, is among the persons whose interrogations are classified Warren Commission documents. Garrison is interested in Alvaredo's testimony. He is not mentioned in the report of the commission.

DEAN ADAMS ANDREWS JR., lawyer and former assistant district attorney of Jefferson Parish, told the Warren Commission a man named Clay Bertrand called him after the assassination of President John F. Kennedy and asked him to defend Lee Harvey Oswald, accused of the shooting. District Attorney Jim Garrison charges that Bertrand is an alias for Clay L. Shaw, who was indicted for conspiracy in the slaying of the President. Andrews said he was unable to say whether Shaw and Bertrand are the same man.

Later, he identified Bertrand as a French Quarter bar owner, Eugene C. Davis. A five-man jury convicted Andrews of perjury on three counts August 9 and he has been sentenced to 18 months in prison.

MANUEL F. ARTIME, Cuban exile leader who commanded the abortive Bay of Pigs invasion, believes Eladio del Valle, a Cuban anti-Castro revolutionist found murdered February 23, 1967, in Miami, was killed at the direction of the Castro regime.

HUGH AYNESWORTH, author of an article in the May, 1967, issue of *Newsweek* Magazine, charged Garrison and his staff with unethical behavior in connection with the DA's Kennedy assassination probe. The article charged that Garrison's had threatened two men and attempted to bribe one of them. Aynesworth, who was working for a Dallas newspaper at the time of the assassination, has spent countless hours on his own investigation, poring through the 26 volumes of the Warren Commission's report and checking lead after lead of his own.

JUDGE BERNARD J. BAGERT, senior judge of Orleans Parish Criminal District Court, ruled after a preliminary hearing for Clay L. Shaw that there was sufficient evidence to hold him for trial on charges of criminal conspiracy in the slaying of Kennedy. Bagert was the presiding member of a special three-judge panel at the hearing.

GUY BANISTER, ex-FBI man and Deputy Chief Superintendent, of Police in New Orleans, had a private detective agency in New Orleans, and employed David W. Ferrie, David F. Lewis, Jack S. Martin, and others, as investigators. Banister died in 1964. The reported cause of death was a heart condition. Witnesses have said that Banister knew Cuban exile leader Sergio Aracha Smith and a man who called himself *Leon* Oswald. Bannister was considered a pivotal figure in the Garrison investigation.

ENDICOTT BATCHELDER, registrar at Tulane University, testified at the preliminary hearing for Clay L. Shaw, accused of criminal conspiracy in the death of the President. He identified some student records of his office. Perry Raymond Russo, the state's star witness at the hearing, once attended Tulane.

ALVIN BEAUBOEUF, a 24-year-old New Orleans man, was one of two men who traveled to Houston, Tex., with David W. Ferrie the day President Kennedy was assassinated. Beauboeuf was arrested in the company of Layton Martens, a former roommate of Ferrie's, by the DA.s office in 1963 in connection with their whereabouts on the day Kennedy was killed. Beauboeuf recently told *Newsweek* Magazine he had been threatened by the DA's office in order to get him to testify in connection with the plot probe. He said he had been offered a bribe and threatened. Beauboeuf was named as heir to Ferrie's estate and a note found in Ferrie's apartment after his death Feb. 22 was addressed "Dear Al:".

MELVIN BELLI of San Francisco, the defense attorney who represented the late Jack Ruby, when Ruby was convicted of slaying accused presidential assassin Lee Oswald, has termed the Garrison investigation unfair. Belli, in a statement May 1 to the San Antonio Trial Lawyers Association, predicted that Garrison's probe will result in convictions on "peripheral charges". Belli said:

"I don't think it's right. It is unfair. I believe the Warren Commission was right."

CLAY BERTRAND is the mystery man who called Dean Andrews after the assassination of President John F. Kennedy and asked him to defend Lee Harvey Oswald, accused of the shooting. The Warren Commission said it was unable to locate Bertrand. District Attorney Jim Garrison charges that Bertrand is an alias for Clay L. Shaw, who was indicted for criminal conspiracy in the slaying of the President. Shaw denies this.

CLEM BERTRAND is the name of the man Perry R. Russo said that he overheard with David W. Ferrie and a man named *Leon* Oswald plotting to kill President Kennedy. He identified Clem Bertrand as Clay L. Shaw, during a preliminary hearing for Shaw.

TOM BETHELL, a London school teacher who came to New Orleans to study the city's traditional jazz, became intrigued with Garrison's assassination probe and asked if he could join the staff. The DA signed him on and assigned him to research the National Archives in Washington. Bethell claims that at least 51 documents vital to the investigation of the assassination have been concealed. He said that 29 of the documents are of special interest to Garrison. Some of the classified Warren Commission documents, he says, indicate the CIA had extensive knowledge of Oswald prior to the assassination of President Kennedy.

U.S. REP. T. HALE BOGGS, D., La., is House Majority Whip. He was one of the seven-man Warren Commission which investigated the slaying of President John F. Kennedy.

MATTHEW S. BRANIFF, Orleans Parish Criminal District Court Judge, was one of a three-judge panel presiding over the preliminary hearing for Clay L. Shaw, accused of criminal conspiracy in the slaying of President John F. Kennedy. Braniff was appointed to the bench by Gov. John J. McKeithen at the insistance of Jim Garrison.

DR. CARLOS BRINGUIER, New Orleans head of the anti-Castro Cuban Student Directorate and a man who has been questioned extensively by Jim Garrison in connection with his probe, has written to the House Committee on Un-American Activities asking the committee to "investigate Mr. Garrison's investigation". Bringuier claims that Oswald was a Communist. He and Oswald got into a scuffle in New Orleans during the summer of 1963 while Oswald was passing out Fair Play for Cuba literature. Both were arrested. Bringuier has filed a defamation suit seeking $1 million in damages against Gambi Publications, Inc., publishers

of the magazine *Saga,* and Harold Weisberg of Hyattstown, Md.,
author of the book, *Whitewash — The Report on the Warren Commission
Report,* and an article in *Saga* dealing with the commission's report.
The suit charges that the book and article defamed Bringuier by
alleging that he was a former official of the Castro government
until he defected in May, 1960; that he disguised his alleged Castro
connections when he testified before the commission and that he is
an enemy of the U.S. who hates this country more than Russia.

MORRIS BROWNLEE, a young New Orleans chemist, describes himself as a godson of the late David William Ferrie.
Brownlee, who is a sort of mystic in an offbeat sect, was extremely
close to the dead pilot. He has been questioned by Garrison.

VERNON B. BUNDY, a Negro narcotics user, testified at the
preliminary hearing for Clay L. Shaw, accused of criminal conspiracy in the slaying of Kennedy, that as Bundy prepared to give himself a "fix" of heroin on the New Orleans lakefront he saw Shaw
with Lee Harvey Oswald during the summer of 1963. Shaw says he
never knew Oswald, whom the Warren commission named as the
lone assassin of the President.

RICHARD V. BURNES, an assistant district attorney in Garrison's office, has been extremely active in the investigation. Garrison said Burnes is the "expert" in the investigation team on the
Dealey Plaza, the assassination site.

JULIAN BUSNEDO, a Cuban exile who participated in the Bay
of Pigs, was a close friend of Sergio Arcacha Smith and knew David
W. Ferrie. Busnedo, now living in Denver, has been questioned in
connection with Garrison's probe. He reportedly met Ferrie here
when he was attempting to get a pilot's license.

EDWARD S. BUTLER, executive director of the anticommunist
Information Council of the Americas described Lee Harvey Oswald
as "a perfect example of a left-wing extremist." He appeared on a
radio debate with Oswald in 1963.

JOHN CAMPBELL, a French Quarter artist and an opera sing-
er, has been questioned by Garrison's office in connection with the
probe, although no indication was given what line the questioning
followed.

JOHN CANCLER, alias "John the Baptist", who gave his occu-
pation as "burglar" and who currently is serving time in the Orleans Parish Prison for burglary, said during a national TV special
produced by NBC that one of Garrison's key witnesses in Clay
Shaw's preliminary hearing, Vernon Bundy, had admitted to him
that he lied on the stand when he testified that he saw Shaw with

Lee Harvey Oswald during the summer of 1963. He also said he was taken to Clay Shaw's house by two members of Garrison's staff and asked if he could break into the house and plant something there.

LUIS CASTILLO, a 24-year-old Puerto Rican, said in Manila in April of 1967 that he was in Dallas to shoot at President John F. Kennedy in 1963. Officials of the Philippine National Bureau of Investigation said that Castillo told them under questioning that he was in Dallas at the time of the assassination and was given a rifle to shoot "a man in an open car". Castillo, according to the *Manila Times,* told NBI investigators that he met an unidentified man in Dallas who took a dismantled rifle from a bowling bag, put it together and gave it to the Puerto Rican. There was no comment on the case from U.S. officials. Dallas police said, when questioned directly by newsmen, they had no record on the man. Santa Fe, New Mexico, records show Castillo has an arrest record for burglary investigation there.

BYRON CHIVERTON, a New Orleans resident, was subpoenaed to appear before the Orleans Parish Grand Jury by Garrison. There has been no explanation of his connection with the DA's probe.

DAVID L. CHANDLER, reporter for *Life* Magazine and one-time close friend of Garrison's. Chandler was closely associated with Garrison during the initial stages of his investigation. He says he became "disillusioned" with the DA's probe primarily because of his actions leading to the arrest of Clay L. Shaw and because of what he termed a misuse of the grand jury by Garrison's office.

DR. NICHOLAS J. CHETTA, Orleans Parish coroner, ruled that David William Ferrie, a key figure in District Attorney Jim Garrison's probe of the assassination died of natural causes. Garrison termed the death a suicide. Dr. Chetta also testified at a preliminary hearing for Clay L. Shaw, accused of criminal conspiracy in the President's death, that he was present when the state's star witness, Perry Raymond Russo, was questioned under hypnosis.

TOMMY CLARK was subpoenaed by Garrison to appear before the Orleans Parish Grand Jury and later was identified as a man Dean Andrews, as assistant Jefferson Parish DA, had paroled for David Ferrie.

MELVIN COFFEY, who formerly lived in Louisiana, was one of two men who traveled to Houston, Tex., with the late David W.

Ferrie the day President Kennedy was assassinated. He is reported not to be considered as a witness in the Garrison investigation.

WILLIAM D. CROWE JR., alias Bill DeMar, performed in Dallas in 1963, doing a mind-reading act. Jack S. Martin, a New Orleans private detective, told the DA's office in 1963 after the assassination that David W. Ferrie knew both Oswald and Ruby and that he may have known Crowe. Ferrie, considered himself a student of hypnotism but staunchly denied knowing Crowe, Oswald or Ruby.

RAYMOND CUMMINGS, a Dallas taxicab driver, came to New Orleans and told the DA's office he had, during 1963, driven Oswald, Ferrie and a third person to the Dallas nightclub of Jack Ruby. Dallas sources report, however, that Cummings did not work for a cab company at that time.

U. S. ATTORNEY GENERAL RAMSEY CLARK first said, after news of Garrison's probe was made public, that Clay L. Shaw had been investigated by the FBI after the assassination and cleared. He then changed his mind and said he had made a mistake, that "nothing arose indicating a need to investigate Mr. Shaw".

WILLIAM DALZELL, described as an international petroleum engineer and consultant and an advisor to the Ethiopian government, was subpoenaed for questioning by Garrison June 30. The subpoena was dropped when Dalzell said he would talk to Garrison voluntarily. Dalzell was an incorporator of a militant anti-Castro organization in New Orleans early in 1961 — the Friends of Democratic Cuba. Joining him as incorporators were Guy Banister, Grady C. Durham and William Klein.

SOL DANN, a Detroit attorney who has represented the Jack Ruby family, wrote to the Louisiana Bar Association in May asking that Garrison be disbarred "for unwarranted and reckless attacks on the Warren Commission's report and its members."

J.B. DAUENHAUER, a New Orleanian and former Army associate of Clay L. Shaw, was Shaw's chief assistant during Shaw's years as managing director of the International Trade Mart. Dauenhauer has been questioned by Garrison's office in connection with the Kennedy probe.

EUGENE C. DAVIS, a French Quarter bartender, was identified by Dean Adams Andrews Jr., the man who first brought up the mysterious Clay Bertrand, as Bertrand to newsmen June 28, 1967. Earlier, Andrews failed to identify Bertrand as Clay L. Shaw, whom Garrison claims used that name as an alias. Davis, however,

does not fit any of the descriptions Andrews had given in the past
of the man he said telephoned him after Kennedy's assassination
and asked him to defend Lee Oswald. Davis denies being Clay Bertrand or ever knowing Oswald.

RICHARDO DAVIS, a New Orleans man who worked with
anti-Castro Cubans who were training for a second invasion of
Cuba at camps near New Orleans in 1963, has been questioned by
Garrison in his probe.

WARREN DeBRUEYS, a former FBI agent at New Orleans
and one of two men called by Garrison to come before the Orleans
Parish Grand Jury and answer questions concerning their investigation of New Orleans aspects of the presidential assassination in
1963. DeBrueys and agent Regis Kennedy were both seen at
anti-Castro Cuban meetings in New Orleans during 1961, according to Cuban sources.

MANUEL CORTES deLARA, a Cuban exile, whose name has
figured in the investigation by Jim Garrison of the Kennedy assassination.

GEORGE AND JEANNE DeMORENSCHILDT were promi-
nent in the White Russian community of Dallas and befriended
and Marina Oswald. Some of their testimony after the assassination have been not been made public. Garrison has expressed interest in their statements, which are classified Warren Commission
documents.

JACK DEMPSEY, *States-Item* reporter, who with David Snyder
and Rosemary James, won the top Associated Press Award in the
two-state area of Louisiana-Mississippi for the original story in
the States-Item February 17, 1967, revealing the Garrison investigation. Dempsey was the first to uncover information leading him
to believe such an investigation was in progress.

OSCAR DESLATTE, a New Orleans truck salesman, was called
before the grand jury by Garrison. Deslatte said he was approached in 1961--before the Bay of Pigs invasion--by two men who
wanted to purchase trucks. He said one of them used the name
Leon Oswald and a purchase offer was made in that name. DA's
office sources pointed out that Lee Oswald was still in Russia and
did not return to New Orleans until early 1963. A bid sheet from
Deslatte's firm with Oswald's name on it was taken as evidence by
the FBI on Nov. 25, 1963--three days after the President's death. It
was not introduced as evidence before the Warren Commission.

DONALD DOOTY, one-time associate of Clay L. Shaw, was

subpoenaed for questioning by District Attorney Jim Garrison in his investigation of the Kennedy murder.

SYLVIA DURAN, a Mexican woman who worked in the Cuban Embassy in Mexico City, was the first person to whom Lee Oswald spoke on his visit to the embassy in 1963. She is quoted extensively in the Warren Report, but Garrison is interested in some of her testimony which is among the classified documents of the Warren Commission.

F. IRVIN DYMOND, a well-known New Orleans criminal lawyer, is chief defense counsel for Clay L. Shaw, under indictment for criminal conspiracy in the slaying of President John F. Kennedy. Dymond was in the race for District Attorney along with Jim Garrison and others in 1961. Dymond was eliminated in the first primary of the race Garrison went on to win.

RANCIER BLAISE EHLINGER, who says he knows Gordon Novel, appeared voluntarily before the Orleans Parish grand jury as it probed the assassination of President John F. Kennedy. Ehlinger, according to his attorney, was in the electronics business with Novel, who is sought by Garrison for questioning in the assassination probe. Ehlinger was arrested as a fugitive from Baton Rouge on an auto theft investigation in 1959. Novel was arrested the same day on the same charge. They were never prosecuted on the charge.

BILL ELDER, WWL-TV, New Orleans, newsman, was subpoenaed and has been questioned before the Orleans Parish Grand Jury in connection with the assassination probe.

MR. and MRS. JULIAN EVANS were landlords to Lee Harvey Oswald and his mother in New Orleans in the mid-1950's. They helped Lee find an apartment when he returned to New Orleans in the spring of 1963. Mr. Evans commented on the "softness" of Oswald's handshake, but Mrs. Evans noted "he carried himself so straight."

HUGH B. EXNICIOS, attorney for the estate of David W. Ferrie, says he will prove Ferrie had nothing to do with the assassination of Kennedy. District Attorney Jim Garrison says Ferrie was a key figure in the assassination plot. Exnicios is a former Republican candidate for district attorney of suburban Jefferson Parish. Exnicios was an attorney for Alvin Beauboeuf and claims he taped a bribe offer to Beauboeuf by Garrison's investigation.

DR. ESMOND FATTER, a New Orleans physician, testified at the preliminary hearing for Clay L. Shaw, accused of criminal conspiracy in the slaying of Kennedy. Fatter was accepted by the court as an expert in hypnotism. He testified that Perry Raymond Russo, the key state witness, was questioned under hypnosis. He also said that Russo was under post-hypnotic suggestion at the time of the hearing.

DAVID WILLIAM FERRIE, a free-lance pilot and private investigator, died Feb. 22, five days after District Attorney Jim Garrison's probe of the death of President Kennedy was made public. Garrison charges that Ferrie conspired with Lee Harvey Oswald and others to kill the President. Ferrie was found dead in his apartment. The coroner's office ruled the death was from natural causes, but Garrison said it was suicide. Ferrie's name first entered the Kennedy case when he and two others were arrested two days after the assassination. They were questioned by the FBI about a trip Ferrie took to Texas the day Kennedy was shot, and released. Ferrie said before his death that he was again questioned by Garrison's office in late 1966 and early 1967. After Ferrie died, Garrison called him "one of the most important individuals in history."

PARMALEE T. FERRIE of Rockford, N.Y., is the brother of David William Ferrie. After Dave Ferrie's sudden death here, he arranged with a New Orleans law firm to handle funeral arrangements. He did not attend the funeral.

ALBERTO FOWLER, a Cuban exile who participated in the Bay of Pigs and who is now director of International Relations for the City of New Orleans, is working with Garrison as an investigator.

MR. AND MRS. JESSE W. GARNER of New Orleans managed the apartment house where Oswald lived in New Orleans in 1963. They were questioned by the Warren Commission, as were Mrs. Edward Boudreaux, and Mrs. Milred Peterman, New Orleans neighbors of the Oswalds; Mrs Bennierita Smith, William E. Wulf and Edward Voebel, former classmates of Oswald when he attended Beauregard Junior High School in 1954.

JIM GARRISON, district attorney of Orleans Parish, says he will prove there was a New Orleans-based conspiracy which culminated in the death of President John F. Kennedy. The tall (6' 6") 46-year-old DA has been a controversial but politically successful figure since taking office in 1961. His political ambitions include a seat in the U.S. Senate. The Kennedy probe has thrust him into the national limelight, though many have criticized his flamboyant methods. Garrison maintains that he has solved the Kennedy murder case and that Lee Harvey Oswald was not the assassin as depicted in the Warren Commission report.

JOHN O. GEORGE, a young New Orleans pipefitter who knew David W. Ferrie and who is a friend of Ferrie's "godson" Morris Brownlee, has been questioned by the DA.

PERSHING GERVAIS, whom Garrison chose as his chief invesgator when he first took office, resigned in 1965 when he became a campaign target of Garrison's opponents. Gervais was one of three top aides of the DA in the old days. The other two, Frank Klein and D'Alton Williams, have worked with Garrison on his investigation, even though they, too, are no longer a part of Garrison's official staff. Gervais, however, who was closest to Garrison, has said he has no interest whatsoever in the case and is in no way involved.

MANUEL GARCIA GONZALES, a Cuban exile, was sought in Miami by the District Attorney's office for questioning in connections with Garrison's Kennedy assassination investigation. Dean Adams Andrews maintains Gonzales is a fictious name invented by himself.

MAX GONZALES, law clerk in Criminal District Judge Frank Shea's court and a pilot, who has worked with Garrison on this investigation. Gonzales, buddy of Garrison's from Army days, has done undercover work for Garrison in the past.

JACK P. F. GREMILLION, Louisiana Attorney General, was asked by the Metropolitan Crime Commission of New Orleans to investigate Garrison's activities in connection with the assassination probe because of numerous allegations of unethical conduct by Garrison's staff. Gremillion refused, saying: "I think this matter ought to be tried in the courts, not in the newspapers, press or TV. I think Mr. Garrison ought to be allowed to try his case in the court."

WILLIAM GURVICH, a partner in a successful New Orleans detective and private guard agency, joined Garrison's staff at the outset of the investigation as his chief investigative aide. He has worked with Garrison on other sensitive investigations and is no stranger to intrigue. Gurvich once posed as a hired gunman while Fort Worth, Tex., detectives listened in on a bizarre plot to have a Texas car dealer murdered. In June, Gurvich quit Garrison abruptly, saying the probe had no basis.

LEONARD and LOUIS GURVICH, brothers of William Gurvich, who defected from Garrison's staff, saying that the investigation has no substance and that charges against Clay Shaw should be dropped, were subpoenaed to appear before the Orleans Parish Grand Jury. All three brothers operate a successful private guard company in New Orleans and are private detectives.

JUDGE EDWARD A. HAGGERTY JR. of the Orleans Parish Criminal District Court has been allotted the trial of Clay L. Shaw on charges of criminal conspiracy in the death of President John F. Kennedy. He has ordered all involved to refrain from pre-trial statements about the case.

RICHARD HELMS, director of the Central Intelligence Agency, was subpoenaed by Garrison's office to produced a "true photograph" of accused presidential assassin Lee Oswald with a burly Cuban, which the DA said was taken by CIA agents in front of the Cuban Embassy in Mexico City in November, 1963. Garrison claimed the photograph was "suppressed" evidence in what he calls a massive cover-up by the CIA and FBI to dupe the Warren Commission and mask the participation of CIA-employed person in the murder of President Kennedy.

LOUIS A. HEYD Jr., Criminal Sheriff of Orleans Parish, has been incharge of courtroom arrangements, including press credentials, for the various hearings that have grown out of District Attorney Jim Garrison's probe of the slaying of President John F. Kennedy. Heyd's office has also figured in the case through serving subpoenas for Garrison and the grand jury.

LEON HUBERT, former Orleans Parish District Attorney and now a Tulane University law professor, was Jim Garrison's boss in the late 1950's when Garrison was an assistant DA. Hubert was a counsel for the Warren Commission, specializing in the investigation of Jack Ruby. He is a former law partner of Malcolm V. O' Hara, who ran against Garrison in 1965 and is now a criminal district Court Judge.

JOSEPHINE HUG, an employee of the International Trade Mart, and a former secretary to Clay L. Shaw, was subpoenaed for questioning by Garrison in connection with the Kennedy probe.

JOHN IRION, a New Orleans man who knew David W. Ferrie when Ferrie was a commander of a Civil Air Patrol squadron, has been questioned by Garrison in his Kennedy investigation.

LOUIS IVON, a young policeman who replaced Pershing Gervais as Garrison's chief investigator, has been active in the Garrison probe. Other investigators on Garrison's staff involved in the probe include Charles Jonau, Kenny Simms, Clancy Navarre, Tom Duffy.

THE REV. CLYDE JOHNSON, preacher and one-time candiate
for governor of Louisiana, has been questioned by Garrison in his
assassination probe. The minister said publicly he was paid by a
man he knew as Alton Bernard to speak against President Kennedy regarding the Bay of Pigs so that Kennedy would be compelled
to visit the South. Johnson said he was told that if enough attacks
were made against Kennedy in the South, the President would be
forced to come South to improve his image. The meeting with Bernard, he said, took place during 1963 at the Roosevelt Hotel. He
identified Bernard as a man about six-foot-two or taller, around
200 pounds, with gray hair. He said Bernard was "very well-
spoken" and appeared to have a "dual personality". He said from
pictures shown on television, he believed that Bernard and Clay L.
Shaw were the same person.

C. W. JOHNSON, district director of the Immigration and Na-
turalization Service in New Orleans, appeared at the preliminary
hearing for Clay L. Shaw, accused of criminal conspircay in the
slaying of President John F. Kennedy. Johnson appeared in re-
sponse to a subpoena by Shaw's attorneys for records on Manuel
Garcia Gonzales and Junio Buzenero.

GUY L. JOHNSON, New Orleans Attorney, was a defense attorney for Clay L. Shaw but withdrew after F. Irvin Dymond became
Shaw's chief defense counsel. Shaw was accused of criminal conspiracy in the slaying of President John F. Kennedy. Johnson in
1963 was defeated by Frank Shea, District Attorney Jim Garrison's
candidate, for a seat on the Criminal District Court bench.

JIMMIE JAMES JOHNSON, a sandy-haired New Orleans
youth, who found the body of the late David W. Ferrie on February
22, 1967. Ferrie was a central figure in Garrison's assassination
inquiry.

PENN JONES, editor of the small Texas newspaper *The Midlothian Mirror,* was the originator of the mysterious deaths or "Kennedy Curse" theory.

DR. JAY KATZ, an associate professor of law and associate professor of clinical psychology at Yale University reviewed two
manuscripts of Perry Russo's questioning by the DA's office. Dr.
Katz concluded during an NBC television special that Dr. Esmond
Fatter, who questioned Russo under hypnosis, asked "very leading
questions" of Russo.

JOHN F. KENNEDY, 35th President of the United States, was
shot to death in Dallas on Nov. 22, 1963.The Warren Commission,
appointed by President Lyndon B. Johnson to investigate Kenne-

dy's death, concluded that the slaying was the work of Lee Harvey Oswald, acting alone. Orleans Parish District Attorney Jim Garrison says the murder was the result of a conspiracy hatched in New Orleans.

REGIS KENNEDY, an FBI agent at New Orleans seen by Cuban sources at meetings in 1961 at New Orleans of anti-Castro groups organized to fight the communist regime of Cuban dictator Fidel ro, was subpoenaed by Garrison's office to appear before the Orleans Parish Grand Jury for questioning. Attorney General Ramsey Clark ordered Kennedy not to go before the jury. Kennedy was also the agent who questioned David W. Ferrie shortly after the assassination of President Kennedy. Judge J. Bernard Bagert ruled that agent Kennedy must go before the Grand Jury. Kennedy showed up but Garrison said later he refused to answer any questions.

SEN. ROBERT F. KENNEDY, D-N.Y., brother of the late President Kennedy, met with William Gurvich who in Washington June 8 reportedly told Kennedy there was no substance to the Garrison investigation. Kennedy expressed confidence in Sheridan of NBC whom Garrison charged with bribery.

JAMES KENNEY, agency director of the Equitable Life Assurance Society, testified at the preliminary hearing for Clay L. Shaw. identifing records of the firm pertaining to Perry Raymond Russo the state's star witness.

BURTON KLEIN, attorney for Alvin Beauboeuf, said he has a tape recording of what he called an attempt by the office of District Attorney Jim Garrison to bribe Beauboeuf, who was a friend of the late David W. Ferrie. Klein is a former assistant DA under Garrison and his predecessor.

FRANK KLEIN, a New Orleans attorney, has been alternately allied with and opposed to District Attorney Jim Garrison. Records indicate he has been helping Garrison in his investigation of the death of Kennedy though he left the DA's office two years ago. He was in the race for district attorney when Garrison was elected in 1961, but was eliminated in the first primary. He announced as a candidate against Garrison in 1965, but withdrew.

HERMAN KOHLMAN, an assistant district attorney under Jim Garrison, was called by private investigator Jack Martin the night of the assassination of Kennedy and told by him that David William Ferrie was involved in the slaying. The call resulted in

Ferrie and two other men being arrested and questioned by Kohl-man and federal agents.

AARON M. KOHN, managing director of the Metropolitan Crime Commission, and E C. UPTON JR., commission president, called on the state attorney general to investigate Garrison's office becuase of charges that the DA's staff had acted unethically in pursuing the investigation of the assassination of President Kennedy.

DAVID R. KROMAN, one of 17 men indicted in a federal fraud and conspiracy trial in connection with an insurance company bankruptcy, said in Bismark, N. D., he has information about the assassination which he plans to reveal.

ALBERT V. LABICHE, was foreman of the Orleans Parish Grand Jury through September, 1967, during a six-month period when Garrison brought a goodly portion of his case before the jury.

AL LANDRY is the "mutual friend" described by Perry Raymond Russo who he said first introduced him to the late David William Ferrie. Russo said he was instrumental in breaking up the friendship between Ferrie and Landry at the request of Landry's parents. Russo was testifying at the preliminary hearing for Clay L. Shaw, accused of criminal conspiracy in the slaying of President John F. Kennedy.

MR. AND MRS. NESTOR LANDRY of 1622 Laurel St., New Orleans, were at Pontchartrain Beach with their children when they were picked up and hauled down to tthe Criminal District Courts building to testify before the Orleans Parish Grand Jury in connection with the Garrison probe. There was no explanation of why they were brought in, but there are strong indications that Mrs. Landry was the one the jury was interested in hearing.

MARK LANE, attorney and author of the controversial best-seller *Rush to Judgement*, which is highly critical of the Warren Commission's investigation and report, has been high in his praise of Garrison's investigation and has been questioned on behalf of the DA's office before the Orleans Parish Grand Jury. Lane, when he attempted to question the much sought after witness in the investigation, Gordon Novel, got into a hot exchange of words with Novel and accused Novel's attorney, Jerry Weiner, of behavior not befitting a lawyer.

GEORGE LARDNER, reporter for the *Washington Post*, was the last person known to have seen David W. Ferrie alive. Lardner told police that he interviewed Ferrie between the hours of midnight and four a. m. February 22, 1967. Ferrie was found dead about noon that day.

FRED LEMANNS, a former New Orleans operator of a turkish bath on Canal Street who now lives in Slidell, said during a national NBC telecast that he had signed a document for Garrison containing the statements that he knew Clay Shaw as Clay Bertrand and that Shaw had frequented his baths in the company of a young man named "Lee". He said the statements were not true and that he had decided he didn't want to "ruin somebody's life on false testimony".

JAMES R. LEWALLEN, an employe of the Boeing Co. at the Michoud Assembly Facility in New Orleans, was a former roommate of David W. Ferrie. He has been questioned by Garrison in connection with the assassination probe.

DAVID F. LEWIS Jr., is a New Orleans shipping clerk for a bus line who says he knew Oswald here in 1963. He has been questioned by District Attorney Jim Garrison in the probe of the slaying of President John F. Kennedy. Lewis says he fears for his life because of what he knows about the assassination plot, but won't disclose the nature of his information.

WESLEY J. LIEBLER, was a Warren Commission attorney who investigated New Orleans aspects of the assassination of Kennedy questioned Dean Andrews in 1964 about his call from "Clay Bertrand" asking him to come to Dallas and defend Lee Harvey Oswald, accused of shooting the President.

JAMES R. LISCOMBE, 30, 0f 708 1/2 Bourbon St., New Orleans, was arrested during the preliminary hearing for Clay L. Shaw, accused of criminal conspiracy in the slaying of President John F. Kennedy. Liscombe, an ex-convict, was booked with making threatening telephone calls after he allegedly called his former warden in Jackson, Mich., and said he was brooding and "intended to make national headlines in New Orleans."

LYNN LOISELL, an investigator attached to Jim Garrison's office and one of the key investigators in the probe, was accused in a *Newsweek* article of attempting to bribe Alvin Beauboeuf, who also accused Garrison's office of threatening him, a statement emphatically denied by Loisell and Garrison.

SEN. RUSSELL B. LONG, D-La., whose own opinions about the shortcomings of the Warren Commission investigation helped to prompt Jim Garrison into an investigation of the Kennedy murder, has spoken out several times on behalf of Garrison and his probe and has pointed out that Garrison has a right and a responsibility to investigate the assassination if he believes that a New Orleans based conspiracy was responsible for the President's death. Long emphasizes that a Presidential murder was not made a federal offense until after Mr. Kennedy's death.

MARLENE MANCUSO, exwife of a material witness in Garrison's probe, Gordon Novel, swore in an affidavit that Novel was in New Orleans in August, 1961, when, Garrison claims, Novel conspired with David Ferrie and Sergio Arcacha Smith to burglarize a munitions bunker near Houma, La. Garrison said in a public statement that Miss Mancuso told him   she was asked by New Orleans newsman Richard Townley of WDSU-TV for a taped interview. Miss Mancuso said, according to Garrison, that Townley told her Garrison was "going to be destroyed". A transcript released by Garrison also quoted Miss Mancuso as saying of Townley, "He gave me the impression that he knows an awful lot about me and that I may as well level with him if I want to be shown in a good light."

IRVING MANN, a New York City cryptographer interviewed by NBC, shed doubt on Garrison's complicated deciphering system which the DA contended yielded the unlisted 1963 phone number of Jack Ruby from numbers found in the notebooks of Clay Shaw and Lee Harvey Oswald.

DANTE MAROCHINI, a young Italian who in 1963 worked for the same New Orleans coffee company as Lee Oswald, was subpoenaed for questioning by the DA's office. Marochini said he knows nothing about Oswald. He now works at the Michoud Assembly Facility of the National Aeronautics and Space Administration. Later, he was arrested on an old bad check charge from North Carolina.

RAY MARCUS, Los Angeles author of *The Bastard Bullet,* has testified before the Orleans Parish Grand Jury as part of Garrison's assassination investigation. Marcus contends that the projectile found on the floor of Parkland Hospital in Dallas could not have struck either Texas Gov. John Connally or President Kennedy.

LAYTON MARTENS, a former roommate of the late David W. Ferrie, a central figure in Garrison's probe, was arrested by the DA's office in 1963 with Ferrie and Alvin R. Beauboeuf. Martens has been questioned extensively by the DA's staff and by the Orleans Parish Grand Jury in connection with the Kennedy probe and was indicted by the jury for perjury.

JACK S. MARTIN, a private investigator, told the FBI that David William Ferrie might be implicated in the assassination of President John F. Kennedy in November, 1963, leading to the arrest of Ferrie and questioning by the FBI several days after the president was slain. The FBI concluded that Martin's charges were baseless.

WILLIAM R. MARTIN, attorney and former director of International Relations for the city's International House, Martin grew up in the Caribbean and is an expert in Latin American affairs and law. He is as fluent in Spanish as he is in English and he worked his way through Tulane Law School as a private investigator. He has joined Garrison's staff as an assistant DA.

JOSEPH S. NEWBROUGH, a one-time close associate of Guy Banister, has been questioned by the DA in his probe.

MIKE MCLANEY, who once operated a gambling casino in Havana, Cuba, and more recently has had a club in Las Vegas, left Cuba after Castro took over. In August of 1963, the FBI raided a cottage in Lacombe, La., near New Orleans, and confiscated a huge each of war materials. The cottage belonged to William Julius McLaney, Mike McLaney's brother. William also lived in Havana and left after Castro took over. The McLaneys said they lent their summer place to a Cuban exile they knew as "Josep Juarez". Juarez was believed to be a name used by Emilio Santana. Mike, a native New Orleanian and a local golf and tennis star at one time, was arrested by the Castro government in 1959, then released and sent a formal letter of apology from Castro's then assistant for American Affairs J. A. Ossorio.

SANDRA MOFFET, now Mrs. Harold McMaines of Omaha, Neb. has been the object of extradition proceedings by District Attorney Jim Garrison's office. Perry Raymond Russo testified that Sandra accompanied him to a party in September, 1963, at which he heard the assassination of President John F. Kennedy plotted. Sandra says she knew Russo, but did not attend that particular party. She also said she did not know Shaw and did not meet Ferrie until 1964. She has moved to Iowa (Garrison's birthplace) which has no extradition agreement with Louisiana.

JOHN MURRET of New Orleans, a cousin of Oswald's, was one of the New Orleanians questioned by the Warren Commission.

LILLIAN MURRET, a sister of Lee Harvey Oswald's mother, let Oswald stay in her home when he returned to New Orleans in April of 1963. He stayed with her until he found a job in May and brought his family in from Texas. She told the Warren Commission

Oswald spent his days job-hunting and his evenings mostly watching television.

GOV. JOHN J. MCKEITHEN of Louisiana has stated that Garrison should be allowed to complete his investigation. To do otherwise, said McKeithen, would be to "confound and confuse the people of the world." McKeithen said that if the state attorney general should stop the probe "as the Metropolitan Crime Commission wants" even more doubts about the President's death would be raised.

GORDON NOVEL, former operator of a French Quarter nightclub and manufacturer of electronic equipment, was a reluctant witness sought by District Attorney Jim Garrison in his probe of the slaying of President John F. Kennedy. Novel left New Orleans while under subpoena to appear before the grand jury, and turned up in Columbus, Ohio, where he termed Garrison's investigation "a fraud." The DA sought to extradite him on the basis of a charge that he (Novel) helped burglarize a Houma munitions bunker in 1961. Garrison has hinted that Novel was connected with the U.S. Central Intelligence agency, and charged that the CIA was paying Novel's attorney. Novel has denied any CIA connections.

MRS. SYLVIA ODIO, a Cuban born woman who fled her country after the Castro take-over was living in Dallas in September of 1963. She was involved with a leftist organization of Cuban refugees known as JURE (Junta Revolucionaria, headed by anti-Castro leader Manolo Ray). Her parents are still in prison in Cuba for JURE activities. She told the Warren Commission that in September, 1963, three men visited her ostensibly to gain membership in JURE. Two were Latins who identified themselves as Leopoldo and Angelo, names which Mrs. Odio called "war names". The third was an American introduced as *Leon Oswald*. Mrs. Odio and her sister said later *Leon* Oswald and Lee Harvey Oswald were the same. The Warren Commission did not highlight her statements in its report, perhaps because of her freely-given statement that she had been under the care of a psychiatrist. Mrs. Odio has since moved to Puerto Rico, where she was visited by Garrison's investigators in an unsuccessful effort to elicit further cooperation from her.

LEE ODOM, a 31-year-old Irving, Tex., man who says he met Clay L. Shaw in New Orleans in November of 1966 when he was in New Orleans to "promote a bullfight", was the man whose name and Dallas address were found in Shaw's addressbook. Odom's address was listed as P.O. 19106. Garrison said the same number, P.O. 19106, was found in Lee Harvey Oswald's notebook, and that the number was in code form the unlisted 1963 telephone number of Jack Ruby.

MALCOLM V. O'HARA, Orleans Parish Criminal District Judge, was one of a three-judge panel presiding over the preliminary hearing for Clay L. Shaw, accused of criminal conspiracy in the slaying of President John F. Kennedy. O'Hara ran against District Attorney Jim Garrison in 1965 when Garrison was seeking his second four-year term DA. O'Hara lost.

ALVIN V. OSER, executive assistant district attorney, was one of the key men in Garrison's office working on the aspects of the case dealing with undercover camps where men were being trained for a Cuban invasion after the Bay of Pigs.

FREDERICK S. O'SULLIVAN, a New Orleans police detective, told the Warren Commission he never found concrete evidence to link Lee Harvey Oswald with David William Ferrie. O'Sullivan knew Oswald in junior high school and was in the Civil Air Patrol with Ferrie. He said Ferrie's plane was checked after the assassination and found not in flyable condition.

JULIUS J. OSWALD, an employee of the Standard Coffee Co., where accused presidential assassin Lee Oswald once was employed, was subpoenaed for questioning by Garrison. He declined to tell newsmen any connection he might have had with Lee Oswald.

LEE HARVEY OSWALD, a New Orleans native who returned to his the city during the summer of 1963, was named by the Warren Commission as the lone culprit in the slaying of President John F. Kennedy in Dallas on Nov. 22, 1963. Oswald was an ex-Marine who had lived in the Soviet Union and proclaimed himself a Marxist, though he became disenchanted with Russian communism. District Attorney Jim Garrison says Oswald was working for the U. S. Central Intelligence Agency, and claims "I have no reason to believe Lee Harvey Oswald killed anybody in Dallas on Nov. 22, 1963."

WILLIAM S. OSWALD of 2704 Wytchwood St. in Metairie, a suburb of New Orleans, was subpoenaed by Garrison for questioning in connection with the probe, but he told newsmen he believed it was a case of mistaken identity. He told reporters that Lee Oswald used his name and address as a reference with Standard Coffee when he applied for a job there in 1963. Oswald says he believes Lee Oswald really meant to use the name of the witness' uncle, another William Oswald, who lives at 136 Elmeer Pl. in Metairie.

MRS. RUTH PAINE is an Irving, Texas,Quaker who befriended Marina Oswald in 1963. The wife of Lee Harvey Oswald stayed with Mrs. Paine during the period April, 1963 before Oswald found work in New Orleans, and again after the family left New Orleans later in the year. In fact, she took the family to Texas while Oswald went to Mexico on Sept. 24. Marina lived with her from then until the day of the assassination of President John F. Kennedy, Nov. 22, 1963. The Warren Commission concluded there was no evidence to suggest that Mrs. Paine or her husband had any connection with the assassination.

SALVATORE PANZECA, a New Orleans attorney, who with the Wegmann brothers and F. Irvin Dymond is a defense attorney for Clay L. Shaw.

ORESTE PENA, a U. S. citizen of Cuban birth, was in 1963 the owner of the Habana Bar, 117 Decatur. He told the Warren Commission Lee Harvey Oswald and an unidentified Mexican came into the bar between 2:30 and 8 one morning between August 15 and August 30.

LEFTY PETERSON, was named by Perry Russo as having attended the party at David Ferrie's house in mid-September, 1963, at which Russo contends a conspiracy to murder the President was hatched by Ferrie, *Leon* Oswald and Clay Shaw. Russo testified during a hearing for Shaw that *Leon* Oswald was Ferrie's roommate. He said *Leon* and Lee Harvey Oswald were the same person. Peterson said on a national television show produced by NBC that Ferrie's roommate at the time of the party was two or three inches taller than himself. Peterson is exactly the same height as Oswald was, five feet, nine inches tall. Peterson also said during the program that no one was present at the party who resembled Clay Shaw.

JAMES PHELAN, writer for the *Saturday Evening Post*, in a story about the Garrison investigation said that Perry Raymond Russo, who testified in court that he knew Clay L. Shaw as "Clem Bertrand", did not make any positive identification of Shaw the first time he was interrogated by the DA's office. Phelan said in the story that he had seen the report made by Assistant DA Andrew J. Sciambra following his initial questioning of Russo. Russo, according to Phelan, did not mention a conspiracy in their first report.

GEORGE PIAZZA II was the attorney for James R. Lewallen, who has been questioned by District Attorney Jim Garrison in his probe of the death of President John F. Kennedy. Lewallen was a former roommate of the late David William Ferrie, a key figure in the probe. Piazza, who was himself a member of the Civil Air Patrol with Ferrie and a close friend, was killed March 30, 1967 in the crash of a Delta Airlines jetliner at New Orleans International Airport.

ORLANDO PIEDRA, former head of the National Police in Cuba under the Batista regime, lived in New Orleans until the Garrison investigation got underway. Piedra's name was mentioned in connection with Garrison probe by Cuban sources.

ED PLANER, news director of WDSU-TV, the New Orleans affiliate of NBC, was subpoenaed to appear before the Orleans Parish Grand Jury for questioning after an NBC special in which NBC claimed that Clay Shaw was not Clay Bertrand, as alleged by Garrison. NBC said they knew the identity of the real Clay Bertrand, described on the program as a well-to-do New Orleans homosexual.

STEVEN R. PLOTKIN is the New Orleans attorney for Gordon Novel, a witness sought by District Attorney Jim Garrison in his investigation of the slaying of President John F. Kennedy. Plotkin also represents Rancier Blaise Ehlinger, a friend of Novel; Jack S. Martin, a private investigator; and David Lewis, a bus line clerk, all of whom have been involved in the investigation. Garrison charged that the bearded Plotkin was being paid by the Central Intelligence Agency for his services as Novel's counsel.

MRS. MARINA OSWALD PORTER, the Russian-born, Russian speaking wife of Lee Harvey Oswald, was held guiltless by the Warren Commission in the assassination of President John F. Kennedy. Marina Nikolaevna Prusakova was a 19-year-old pharmacist when she married Oswald on April 30, 1961 in Minsk. She was the niece of a Soviet MVD official. She returned to the U.S. with Lee. They had two children. After the assassination she married another American citizen and has remained in this country.

CARLOS QUIROGA, a former close associate of Sergio Arcacha Smith, who led the Cuban Democratic Revolutionary Front, an anti-Castro group, in New Orleans in 1961 and a fugitive from Garrison's inquiry, was questioned by Garrison on several occasions, including testimony before the Orleans Parish Grand Jury. Quiroga claimed he had "proof" Lee Oswald was a Communist.

LUIS RABEL, a Cuban exile, who has figured prominently in New Orleans activities of an anti-Castro nature, has been questioned by Garrison.

I. T. (TROY) RACKLEY of Emory, Tex., according to an article
in the *Houston Post* of Sunday, March 5, 1967, was a patron of Jack
Ruby's Carousel Club in Dallas November 8, 1963. Rackley saw
Ruby with a man, whom a waitress called by a name that sounded
like "Bettit" or "Pettit". Rackley later told the FBI that the man
he had seen with Ruby resembled Lee Oswald. Garrison, according
to the Post Article, was said to believe that the man "Bettit" or
"Pettit" was David W. Ferrie, a central figure in the Garrison
probe. However, Ferrie and Oswald were nothing alike in age or
appearance. The FBI, which said it proved Oswald was somewhere
else at the time, discounted Rackley's testimony.

JOSEPH RAULT Jr., wealthy New Orleans oilman, was instrumental in forming a group known as "Truth and Consequences,
Inc." made up of some 50 businessmen devoted to financing Garrison's Kennedy investigation so he would not have to reveal his
movements in the probe through expense vouchers which are
public record. Garrison first became seriously interested in conducting his own investigation after a conversation with Rault and
Louisiana Sen. Russell B. Long, who expressed to him some of
their own doubts about the Warren Commission's conclusions.

JOHN F. REILLY, a technician for the Police Bureau of Identification, testified at the preliminary hearing for Clay L. Shaw,
accused of criminal conspiracy in the death of President John F.
Kennedy. Reilly identified a photograph he said he took of the
front of the apartment of the late David William Ferrie, a key figure in District Attorney Jim Garrison's investigation of the President's death.

DELPHINE ROBERTS, secretary of the late Guy Banister, has
been questioned extensively by Garrison's office in connection with
the investigation.

WILLARD E. ROBERTSON, influential in the New Orleans
business world as a Volkswagen importer, a key figure in the financial end of Louisiana politics and a political ally of Jim Garrison,
was one of the businessmen instrumental in forming an organization known as "Truth and Consequences, Inc.," a group of some 50
men who are giving Garrison financial support for his investigation were made known through an examination of public expense
records. The group has pledged indefinite support of the investigation so Garrison can conduct it in secrecy.

EVARISTO RODRIGUEZ, a Cuban who came to this country in
1962, was a bartender at the Habana Bar, 117 Decatur, in August
of 1963. He told the Warren Commission that at that time Lee

Harvey Oswald and an unidentified Mexican came into the bar between 2:30 and 3 one morning between Aug. 15 and Aug. 30. He said Oswald ordered a lemonade and complained about paying 25 cent for it. He said Oswald appeared drunk.

JACK RUBY, a Dallas nightclub owner, shot Lee Harvey Oswald to death in the Dallas police station two days after President John F. Kennedy was assassinated. The Warren Commission investigated Ruby extensively and found no previous connection between him and Oswald, but District Attorney Jim Garrison claims he has found a coded form of Ruby's unpublished telephone number in an Oswald diary. Ruby was tried and convicted of the slaying of Oswald, but won a new trial and was awaiting it in the Dallas County jail when he died of cancer early in 1967.

PERRY RAYMOND RUSSO, a 25-year-old Baton Rouge insurance salesman, was the star witness for District Attorney Jim Garrison in the preliminary hearing for Clay L. Shaw, who is accused of criminal conspiracy in the slaying of President John F. Kennedy. Russo testfied that he heard Shaw, Lee Harvey Oswald and David William Ferrie plot the assassination in September of 1963. He dramatically pointed to Shaw in the courtroom as the man he knew as Clay Bertrand. It was brought out later in the hearing that Russo was testifying while under posthypnotic suggestion.

EUGENE SANNER, 29, was recently extradited from New Orleans to Illinois, where he was wanted on four counts of burglary, told Garrison he had information that Ferrie and Oswald were once in Illinois together gathering funds for an invasion of Cuba. Sanner, before being extradited, was being held in Parish Prison. He planned a mass escape from Parish Prison. When the escape attempt finally was made Sanner already had been transferred. The escape was foiled and all were caught, but Sanner was charged with planning the break anyhow.

EMILO SANTANA, a Cuban exile, who received a suspended sentence on a New Orleans burglary charge and was on probation under a Miami parole officer, was brought to New Orleans the week of February 14 for questioning by Garrison's office, in connection with the probe.

EDDIE L. SAPIR, New Orleans city councilman, is an attorney for Gordon Novel, a witness sought by District Attorney Jim Garrison in his probe of the slaying of President John F. Kennedy. Sapir's family also owns the house in which David William Ferrie, had rented an apartment for several years. The Shaw, Ferrie, Oswald assassination plot is supposed to have taken place in this apartment in mid-September, 1963. Ferrie died there on Feb. 22, 1967.

OLIVER P. SCHULINGKAMP, Orleans Parish criminal district judge, has been allotted the trial of Layton Patrick Martens on a perjury charge in connection with an investigation of a Houma munitions theft. Martens is a former roommate of the late David William Ferrie, a key figure in District Attorney Jim Garrison's probe of the slaying of President John F. Kennedy. Schulingkamp was one of the eight judges in the spectacular feud with Garrison in 1963 over Garrison's use of the fines and fees fund to finance investigations.

PETER SCHUSTER, a photographer for the Orleans Parish Coroner's office, testified at the preliminary hearing for Clay L. Shaw, accused of criminal conspiracy in the death of President John F. Kennedy. Schuster identified certain photographs he said he had taken of the apartment of the late David William Ferrie, a key figure in District Attorney Jim Garrison's investigation of the President's death.

ANDREW J. SCIAMBRA, one of Garrison's assistant DAs, was the first to question Perry Russo, the DA's chief witness in his charge against Clay Shaw. *Saturday Evening Post* writer James Phelan, in an article, wrote that the first time Russo was questioned he did not mention to Sciambra anything about a party at which a conspiracy was hatched. Sciambra said that Phelan was confused and he was willing to match facts against Phelan before the Orleans Parish Grand Jury and challenged Phelan to appear with him.

CLAY L. SHAW, former managing director of the International Trade Mart, is under indictment for criminal conspiracy in the slaying of President John F. Kennedy. Shaw, 54, denies any connection with any conspiracy. Perry R. Russo, a witness called by District Attorney Jim Garrison at a preliminary hearing for Shaw, testified that he heard Shaw, Lee Harvey Oswald and David W. Ferrie plotting the assassination in September, 1963.

FRANK J. SHEA, Orleans Parish Criminal District Judge, was alotted the trial of Dean Andrews for perjury in connection with District Attorney Jim Garrison's probe of the slaying of President John F. Kennedy. Shea was elected with Garrison's support, but since has broken with the DA.

DR. MARY STULTS SHERMAN, nationally known orthopedic surgeon, was stabbed to death and partially burned in her apartment at 3101 St. Charles Ave. on July 21, 1964. The man who found the body was Juan M. Valdes, a self-described Latin playwright who also lived in the apartment building. On May 24, 1967, he was subpoenaedby District Attorney Jim Garrison in connection with Garrison's probe of the slaying of President John F. Kennedy. No explanation was given for calling Valdes.

WALTER SHERIDAN, a key member of the NBC team sent to New Orleans to do a special on Garrison's investigation, has been accused by Garrison of tampering with a witness in his case, Perry Raymond Russo. Garrison, who describes Sheridan as a "former investigator for the federal government", said Sheridan had directed an attempt by NBC to destroy his case. He said Sheridan tried to induce Russo to go to California and telling Russo NBC would take care of all of his expenses. Garrison complained of Sheridan's actions in a letter to the Federal Communications Commission and charged him with public bribery.

DAVID SNYDER, *States-Item* reporter, who with Rosemary James and Jack Dempsey, also of the *States-Item,* collected the information for the story in the *States-Item* February 17, 1967, revealing that Garrison was investigating the Kennedy assassination. Snyder who has been with the newspaper for eight years, is the City Hall columnist.

LAWRENCE SOLOW, was a partner of Gordon Novel in the New Orleans night spot, the Jamaican Village, before Novel fled New Orleans.

FRANK J. STASS, 51,of 400 Faye ave., Metairie, registrar at Loyola University, testified at the preliminary hearing for Clay L. Shaw, accused of criminal conspiracy in the slaying of the President. He identified records pertaining to Perry R. Russo, the state's star witness at the hearing, who once attended Loyola.

WILLIAM KIRK STUCKEY, a newsman and expert on Latin American Affairs, interviewed Lee Harvey Oswald on radio in New Orleans during the summer of 1963. On one of the programs, Oswald proclaimed himself a Marxist. Stuckey said of Oswald: "He was a nice guy. I liked him. I felt sorry for him, too."

KERRY THORNLEY, a novelist, served in the Marine Corps with Lee Harvey Oswald, named by the Warren Commission as the lone assassin of President John F. Kennedy. Thornley wrote a book which included an Oswald-like character, and gave the Warren Commission extensive testimony of Oswald's Marine days. He said he is "not sure" Oswald committed the assassination.

BERNARDO TORRES, a Cuban exile living in Miami, once

helped to guard President Kennedy during a speaking appearance in Miami. Torres has been working with Garrison on his investigation of the Kennedy murder and says that Garrison's investigation will make the Warren Commission investigation look pale.

MIGUEL TORRES, a Cuban exile who was arrested and sentenced to the Louisiana State Penitentiary at Angola for burglary, was transferred to Parish Prison (county jail) by Garrison's office for questioning in connection with the Kennedy investigation. Torres is believed to be a source of information about others rather than a material witness to the investigation.

RICHARD TOWNLEY, WDSU-TV, New Orleans, newsman was subpoenaed and appeared for questioning by the Orleans Parish Grand Jury in connection with the Garrison probe. Later, Perry Raymond Russo, a key witness for the prosecution in Garrison's case against Clay L. Shaw, said publicly that Townley, NBC reporter Walter Sheridan and *Saturday Evening Post* writer James Phelan made repeated visits to his home to try and persudae him to appear on NBC's documentary on the Garrison case. Russo quoted Townley as saying the NBC group was working with Shaw's defense in an effort to wreck the state's case. NBC and WDS-TV denied these statements. Garrison has charged Townley with public bribery and intimidation of a witness.

WILLIAM TURNER, a former FBI man and now a writer, was subpoenaed and appeared before the Orleans Parish Grand Jury. Turner was the author of an article in *Ramparts* magazine which flatly declared there was a well-organized conspiracy to kill Kennedy in Dallas.

JUAN M. VALDES, who describes himself as a Latin playwright, was subpoenaed on May 24, 1967, to appear at District Attorney Jim Garrison's office in connection with Garrison's investigation of the slaying of President John F. Kennedy. Garrison would give no reason for calling Valdes. Valdes was in the news in 1964 when he discovered the body of a slain woman physician, Dr. Mary Stults Sherman, at the apartment building where they both lived.

ANGEL VEGA, a Cuban exile, who lives in Miami, has been questioned by Garrison in connection with his investigation.

EDWARD VOEBEL, once a classmate of Oswald's in a New Orleans junior high school, said shortly after the assassination in an interview that he believed Oswald had been in the Civil Air Patrol under the command of David W. Ferrie. Since Garrison's investigation was initiated, however, Voebel has refused to confirm his earlier statement.

BRECK WALL, an entertainer who worked at Ruby's nightclub, went to Galveston shortly after the assassination, as did David William Ferrie. Wall talked to Ruby for two minutes by telephone from Galveston at 11:44 the night before Ruby killed Oswald.

CHARLES RAY WARD, Garrison's First Assistant DA, who like Garrison has political ambitions and who like Garrison smokes a pipe. Ward may want to be the next district attorney of Orleans Parish.

EDWARD F. AND WILLIAM J. WEGMANN, New Orleans attorneys and brothers, represent Clay L. Shaw along with F. Irvin Dymond, chief defense counsel. Edward Wegmann has been Shaw's attorney for 20 years. Shaw is under indictment for criminal conspiracy in the slaying of President John F. Kennedy.

JERRY WEINER, a Columbus, Ohio, attorney, represented Gordon Novel in his efforts to avoid extradition from that state. Novel was sought by District Attorney Jim Garrison to testify in his investigation of the slaying of President John F. Kennedy. Weiner attempted to silence Novel at a news conference as Novel described a burglary of a Houma munitions bunker in which he is accused of participating as "one of the most patriotic burglaries in history."

HAROLD WEISBERG, New York author of two books severely critical of the Warren Commission Report on President Kennedy's death, testified before the Orleans Parish Grand Jury. He told newsmen later that "District Attorney Garrison's investigation is going to culminate in a congressional investigation." He wrote *Whitewash* and *Whitewash II*.

DR. RONALD A WELSH, who performed the autopsy on the body of David William Ferrie, said anatomical findings indicated that Ferrie did not commit suicide, but died of a ruptured blood vessel at the base of the brain. District Attorney Jim Garrison, who calls Ferrie a key figure in his probe of the death of President John F. Kennedy, says Ferrie's death was a suicide.

D'ALTON WILLIAMS, New Orleans attorney who worked with Garrison in 1962 as the DA's chief administrative aide, then left to go into private practice, has worked with Garrison on his Kennedy investigation.

O. M. WRIGHT, a friend of Clay L. Shaw, became enraged the night of Shaw's arrest when newsmen and photographers gathered outside Shaw's French Quarter home to watch the DA's men search the premises. He struck photographer Irby Aucoin, who has charged Wright with assault.

SAM MONK ZELDEN, attorney for Dean Andrews, was called by Andrews the Sunday after President John F. Kennedy was slain in Dallas on Friday, Nov. 22, 1963. Andrews, then confined to a hospital, asked Zelden to go to Dallas and represent Lee Harvey Oswald, accused of shooting the President, until Andrews was well enough to take over. Before Zelden could make up his mind, Oswald was shot to death by Jack Ruby. Zelden represented Andrews until the day of his perjury trial. He withdrew, saying he and Andrews could not agree on strategy. Andrews defense was taken up by three Jefferson Parish brothers, Harry, Cecil and Bruce Burglass.